Healthy
Lao Cuisine
Tasty and Easy to Make

Sum Sap
(enjoy your meal)

Penn Hongthong

Other books by Penn Hongthong:

Simple Laotian Cooking

Legwork Team Publishing
New York

Legwork Team Publishing

80 Davids Drive, Suite One

Hauppauge, NY 11788

www.legworkteam.com

Phone: 631-944-6511

ISBN: 978-0-578-02845-3 (sc)

First edition 6/16/2009

Printed in the United States of America

This book is printed on acid-free paper

Legwork Team
Publishing

To my heart and soul, my daughter, Soutara Hongthong:

Your birth woke me up from being lifeless.

For you, I worked harder and wanted more.

If not for you, I would not be where I am.

To my sister, Likavanh Voice:

A special thank you for always being supportive and believing in me.

To my maternal grandmother, Soth Hongthong:

For not kicking me out of your kitchen and garden.

To my mother, Phanh Hongthong:

For having me do all the prep work, which reinforced my interest in cooking.

To my beloved paternal grandmother, Dang Hongthong:

For your love and fairness.

Acknowledgments

Much appreciation is directed to my family, especially those to whom this book is dedicated. Their influence on my life is reflected in the healthy food recipes I can share with you today.

Producing a book of this quality, could only become a reality through the dedicated efforts of Yvonne Kamerling and Janet Yudewitz of Legwork Team Publishing. I extend my gratitude to them, and as the name implies, their team of design, editorial and technical professionals for transforming my ideas into the beautiful volume you hold in your hands. Thank you so much Suzanne Travan for designing a beautiful book for me, it is beyond my expectation and I am very grateful for your patience.

I gratefully acknowledge the following individuals for using their creative photography skills to further enhance the quality of this book:

Special thanks to Lynn Spinnato, Port Jefferson, NY for the sensitive Cover photos of me and my daughter. You can see more of Lynn's captivating photography by personally visiting her Gallery in Port Jefferson, NY or by viewing her web site: www.spinnatogallery.com.

Additional special thanks to Dr. Kim W. Bridges for the superb Plumeria photos appearing on the Cover. Professor Bridges, Botany Department, University of Hawaii, Manoa has done extensive research on conservation in Laos. Additional photos of this national flower can be found at: www.botany.hawaii.edu/faculty/bridges/Plumeria/gsize/backgrounds2.htm.

Thank you to Randy Handwerger, Animal Photographer & S. S. Aqua Dog Swimmer, East Hampton, NY for the Steamer Set and Steamer Basket photos. More of Randy's artistry can be seen at: www.RandyProductions.com.

Successful businesses rely on supportive associates for continued ideas, growth and market share. I want to especially thank the production crew at LTV East Hampton, NY: Robert Frank, Seth Redlus, Patrice Jacobsen, and Lee Davis for their creative taping of my cooking show Simple Lao Cuisine. Visit my web site (www.simplelaocuisine.com) and also check their web site for further details: www.ltveh.org.

I was born and grew up in Paklay, Sayaboury, Laos, located in Southeast Asia—a landlocked country between China, Burma, Thailand, Cambodia and Vietnam. The only thing my maternal grandmother and I had in common was cooking and gardening. She grew garden vegetables, leafy vegetables such as: lettuce, bok choy, Chinese broccoli, and water spinach by the lake and along the Mekong riverbank—I loved her vegetables and she loved my help watering her vegetables by carrying water from the lake and the river. Afterward, she would pick bok choy, dill, garlic leaves, scallions, and cilantro and wash them at the lake or in Mekong River. I loved the aroma of her herbs while washing them. Once the vegetables and herbs were clean, I would carry them in a bamboo basket back home for my mother to cook for dinner.

My beloved paternal grandmother lived a quarter mile away; she grew farm vegetables, fruit like vegetables such as: eggplants, winter squash, wax gourds, sponge gourds, ridge gourds, okra and much more. After school, I would ride my bicycle to her farm, pick the best vegetables, and bring them home for my mother to cook. She said, "We eat only the young and best ones; the old and ugly ones, we sell." My sister, Likavanh, and I went to the farm with her on the weekends. We looked forward to the vegetable soup made with baby eggplants, baby sponge gourds (mock borb), baby ridge gourds (mock noy), baby wax gourds (mock mone lane), winged beans (mock tore pou), baby winter squash (mock ur noy), and grape eggplants (mock kang). While Likavanh and I wanted to rush and pick the vegetables for lunch, my maternal grandmother said, "Wait until lunchtime. We'll get the pot going first, and then we'll pick the vegetables. They'll go right into the pot, and they'll taste sweet and fresh."

I hated getting up early to go to the market, but I could not miss finding out what vegetables and meats were available in the market that day. If I didn't get up early enough, it would be a very boring day—only pork and leftover vegetables. Farmer's wives and children had to sell everything before going to their rice farms. If I got to the market early enough, there were so many varieties of fruit and vegetables, changing with the season, and our food was never boring.

Lao cuisine is already extremely healthy. I recreated these recipes to make them even healthier, as well as simplifying them to make them easier to prepare, while still keeping the original flavors.

In Lao cooking, meats, fish, and poultry are used to flavor the vegetables. In Laos, freshwater fish were plentiful and tasted less fishy than ocean fish. The only seafood we had access to was steamed mackerel, imported from Thailand. Shrimp from the Mekong River and crabs from rice paddies or ponds were small and eaten whole.

Bread and dairy products are not a typical part of Lao cuisine. The only grain used in Lao cuisine is rice—rice for breakfast, lunch, and dinner. Noodles and wrappers are typically made from rice flour.

Fresh ingredients are very important to our Lao cuisine, especially the fresh herbs. By using large amounts of fresh herbs, a lot of flavor is added to the food and it balances out when served with plain rice and vegetables.

When I arrived in New York, my sister Likavanh very excitedly introduced me to everything. She showed me the refrigerator, saying, "We have a refrigerator full of food: juice, milk, soda, fruits and vegetables all the time. We can eat and drink anything as much as we want." It was unbelievable to me. She went on. "We go food shopping once a week and keep them in the refrigerator." I asked, "Not every morning like at home in Laos?" We got to the supermarket and she showed me the produce section first because she knew that I liked vegetables. Everything was neatly packed, labeled, and priced. I thought they were just for show; the size of the vegetables was so much larger, I didn't think they were real.

My first meal was roasted beef. I asked my mother, "That giant piece of meat is for dinner?" a piece of meat that size would feed my whole town. My excitement was overwhelming to have a whole piece of meat on my plate, but I was disappointed with my first bite. There were no explosive flavors of garlic, lemongrass, soy sauce, fish sauce, or fresh herbs. "Maybe my sponsor forgot to add flavor," I told myself. The next night we had a roasted whole chicken. I had never seen a whole chicken on the dinner table in all my life. One chicken was cut up in bite-sized pieces and cooked with a lot of vegetables; this would make four meals for my large family of nine children, parents, and grandmother. In my hometown in Laos at the food stall, each chicken leg or breast was clipped between split bamboo pieces, roasted over a fire, and based with an incredible flavor. The aroma filled the air. I had dreamed of having a whole leg of chicken for myself for seventeen years. Now at the age of eighteen, I finally got to eat a leg of chicken. I think everybody noticed my excitement. I took a bite and got very confused. What happened to the flavor? Something was wrong. I didn't speak any English, so I couldn't say anything.

I cooked my own food after school and enjoyed adding a lot of different meats. I was eighteen, in a strange world, didn't speak the language, and I didn't know anything. So I cooked and ate a lot of meat and had a lot of ice cream; those were the only good things in my life at that very difficult time. Three or four months later, I was done with meat; I needed my rice and vegetables. Then I started to notice that many Americans are overweight, eat a lot of meat and very little vegetables. It took me a long time to figure it out. I thought back to my first and second American meals. I didn't like the meats or the vegetables because there were no flavors. Americans eat a lot of meat to feel full and no vegetables because they don't taste good. I started to think about what I could do. Original Lao recipes take too long because everything is made from scratch. The flavor is made very strong to balance out when served with plain rice and vegetables.

I had to find a way to simplify the recipes so they would still taste original by:

- Making the entrée and vegetable side dish taste good, but not overpowering to scare first-timers so people will eat both.
- Eliminating unnecessary ingredients (because there are too many ingredients) still maintaining original taste.

- Modifying the recipes with using only meat. Americans eat only the meaty parts: no bones, innards, or other parts of animals. This was very hard because Lao cooking discards almost nothing of the animal parts, and believes that all parts of the animal make the food taste good. Without them, I couldn't see how I would make my recipes taste as good.

My bigger problem was that I had to cut out MSG. Lao cooking is concentrated on getting more with the little you have and getting help from MSG to make the food taste good. MSG is used in most Asian cooking.

After trying and trying for years, I came up with some solutions. I realized that it's all about balance and proportion: more meat than original Lao cooking and less than American cooking; less vegetables than Lao original cooking and more than American cooking.

It's also about cooking a small amount: the right amount of meat to flavor the right amount of vegetables, and a large amount of herbs and spices to replace the MSG.

SURN SAP

(Enjoy your meal.)

ພຽງເພັນ ທິງທອງ

Penn Hongthong

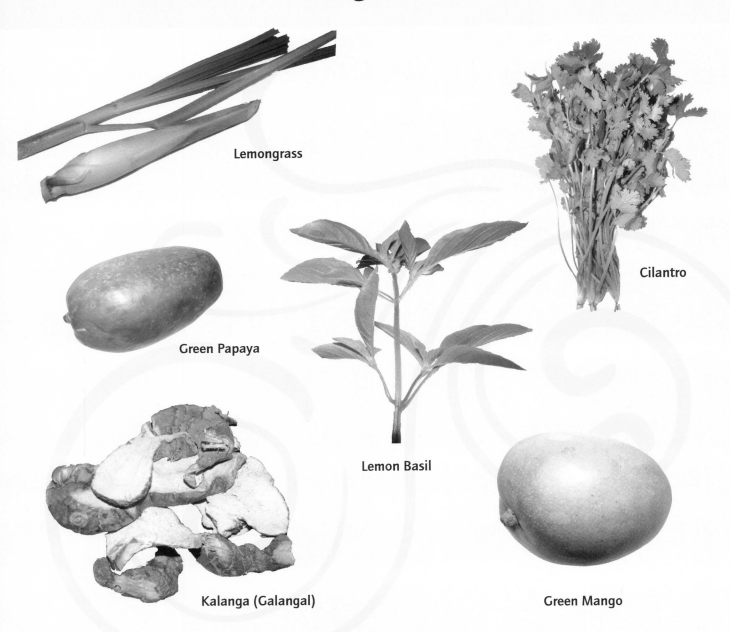

Lemongrass

Cilantro

Green Papaya

Lemon Basil

Kalanga (Galangal)

Green Mango

For more information about the ingredients, brand and where to purchase, go to Penn Hongthong's web site www.laochef.com

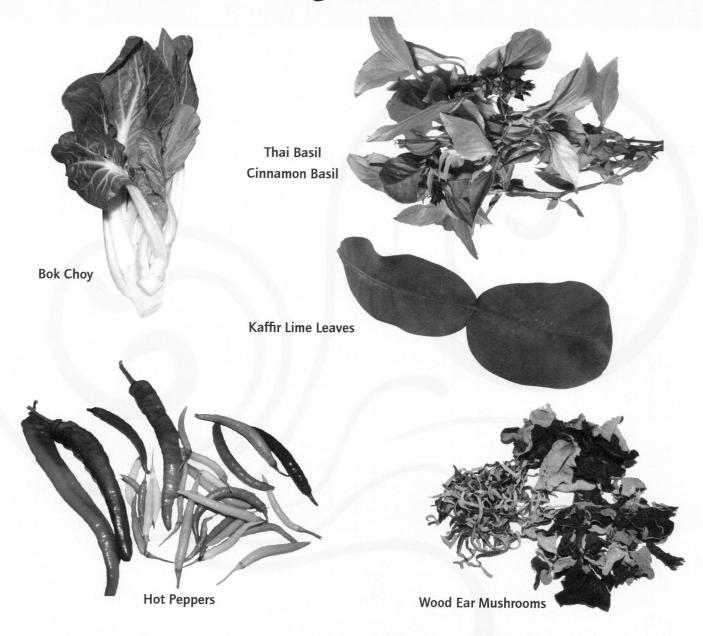

Thai Basil
Cinnamon Basil

Bok Choy

Kaffir Lime Leaves

Hot Peppers

Wood Ear Mushrooms

For more information about the ingredients, brand and where to purchase, go to Penn Hongthong's web site www.laochef.com

Ingredients

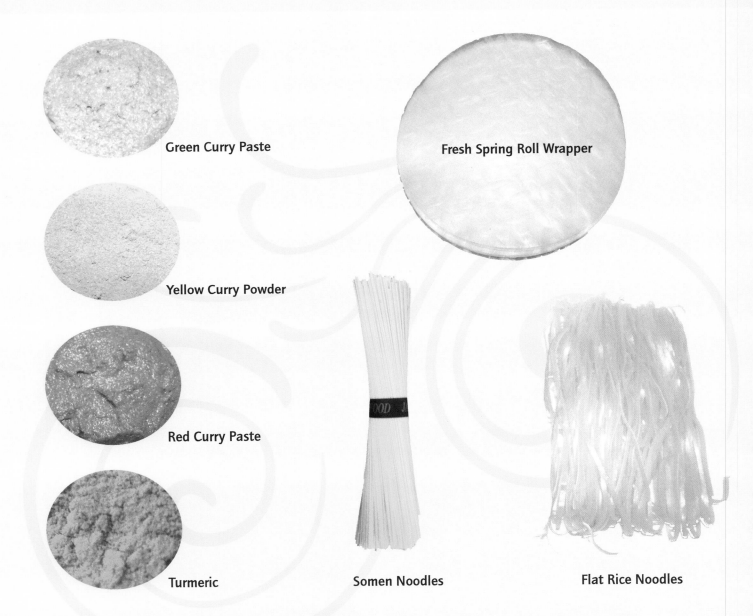

Green Curry Paste

Fresh Spring Roll Wrapper

Yellow Curry Powder

Red Curry Paste

Somen Noodles

Flat Rice Noodles

Turmeric

For more information about the ingredients, brand and where to purchase, go to Penn Hongthong's web site www.laochef.com

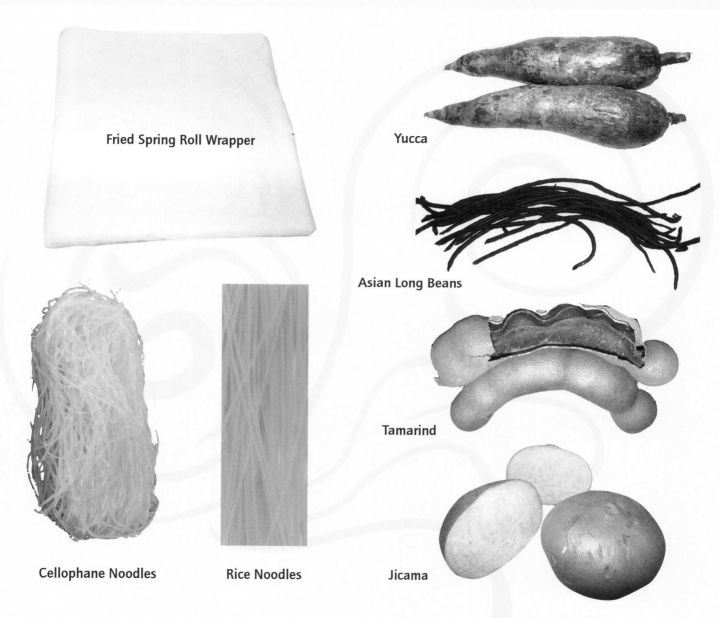

Fried Spring Roll Wrapper

Yucca

Asian Long Beans

Tamarind

Cellophane Noodles

Rice Noodles

Jicama

For more information about the ingredients, brand and where to purchase, go to Penn Hongthong's web site www.laochef.com

RICE

STICKY (OR SWEET) RICE
(Kao Neal)

You will need a special steamer basket and pot to cook sticky rice.

When buying the rice, make sure to ask for sticky (or sweet) rice from Thailand. If you ask for sticky rice, many people will not know what it is. If you ask for sweet rice, most people will think you are asking for Japanese sweet rice, which is used to make sushi.

2 cups sticky (or sweet) rice

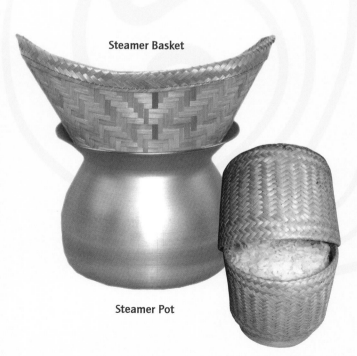

Steamer Basket

Steamer Pot

Sticky Rice Container

Soak the rice in warm water for at least 2 hours (4 hours is better). Fill a steamer pot with 4 cups of water and place it on the stove over high heat.

Strain the rice into a steamer basket, rinsing well and draining off the excess water. Place the steamer basket over the steamer pot, making sure the bottom of the basket does not touch the water. Cover the rice (use any pot lid that fits) and steam over high heat for 15 to 20 minutes until the rice is cooked (it will turn clear). Remove the basket from the pot, and stir with a wet wooden spoon and then transfer the rice to a sticky rice container.

Serves 2.

Note: *Sticky rice must be kept in a bamboo container, as it allows the steam to escape while keeping the rice warm. Excess moisture will make the rice soggy and cause it to stick to your hands. Sticky rice should be eaten by hand, so have fun playing with your food!*

BASIL SHRIMP FRIED RICE
(Kore Kao Bore La Pa)

2 tablespoons olive oil

4 cloves garlic, minced

1 tablespoon finely minced ginger

¼ pound shrimp, peeled and cleaned

¼ teaspoon salt

1 egg white

¼ teaspoon turmeric

1 cup coarsely chopped snow peas

¼ cup coarsely chopped red onion

1 tablespoon soy sauce

2 cups cooked rice

¼ teaspoon ground white pepper

¼ cup coarsely chopped scallions

½ cup coarsely chopped Thai or any basil

Heat a wok or frying pan with olive oil over high heat. Add the garlic and ginger, stirring constantly for 30 seconds or until light brown. Add the shrimp and salt, stirring well for 1 minute.

Lightly beat egg the white with the turmeric and then add to the wok, wait 30 seconds, and then mix lightly, not completely stirring in the egg mixture. Add the snow peas, onion, and half of the soy sauce, stirring well for 1 minute. Turn the heat down to medium, and add the rice, white pepper, and the remaining soy sauce, stirring constantly for 2 minutes. Add the scallions and basil, stir well, and serve hot.

Serves 2.

CHICKEN FRIED BROWN RICE
(Kore Kao Gice)

2 tablespoons olive oil

4 cloves garlic, minced

1 tablespoon finely minced ginger

¼ pound ground chicken

¼ teaspoon salt

1 egg white

¼ teaspoon turmeric

1 cup coarsely chopped purple cabbage

½ cup coarsely chopped onion

1 tablespoon soy sauce

2 cups cooked brown rice

¼ teaspoon ground black pepper

¼ cup coarsely chopped scallions

¼ cup coarsely chopped cilantro

Heat a wok or frying pan with olive oil over high heat. Add the garlic and ginger, stirring constantly for 30 seconds or until light brown. Add the chicken and salt, stirring constantly until the liquid has evaporated—about 2 minutes.

Lightly beat the egg white with the turmeric and then add to the wok, wait 30 seconds, and then mix lightly, not completely stirring in the egg mixture. Add the cabbage, onion, and half of the soy sauce, stirring well for 1 minute. Turn the heat down to medium, and add the rice, black pepper, and the remaining soy sauce, stirring constantly for 2 minutes. Add the scallions, stir well, and turn off the heat. Add the cilantro, stir lightly, and serve hot.

Serves 2.

SPICY MINT FRIED RICE
(Kore Kao Pit)

Any type of hot peppers can be used, including: habanero, chili, long hot, and jalapeño (listed from hottest to most mild).

2 tablespoons olive oil

4 cloves garlic, minced

1 tablespoon finely minced ginger

¼ pound ground turkey

¼ teaspoon salt

1 teaspoon hot pepper flakes or chopped hot peppers

1 ½ cup cucumbers, cut into ½ inch cubes

1 tablespoon soy sauce

2 cups cooked rice

½ cup coarsely chopped scallions

½ cup coarsely chopped fresh mint

Heat a wok or frying pan with olive oil over high heat. Add the garlic and ginger, stirring for 30 seconds or until light brown. Add the ground turkey and salt, stirring constantly until the liquid has evaporated—about 2 minutes. Add the hot pepper flakes, cucumber and half of the soy sauce, stirring well for 1 minute. Turn the heat down to medium, and add the rice and the remaining soy sauce, stirring constantly for 2 minutes. Add the scallions, stir well, and turn off the heat. Add the mint, stir lightly, and serve hot.

Serves 2.

HONEY PEANUT SAUCE
(Jail Tore Din)

½ cup honey or brown sugar
1 teaspoon salt
1 tablespoon fish sauce

1 clove garlic
¼ cup peanut butter
2 tablespoons lime or lemon juice

Combine all ingredients in a blender. Add 1 cup of water and blend for 30 seconds or until creamy. Refrigerate in an airtight container for up to a week or freeze for up to 3 months.

Serve with fresh spring rolls, fried spring rolls, or as a salad dressing.

Serves 4.

SATAY SAUCE
(Num Satay)

1 tablespoon olive oil
1 teaspoon yellow curry powder
½ cup coconut milk
1 tablespoon brown sugar

½ teaspoon salt
2 tablespoons peanut butter
1 tablespoon tamarind concentrate or lime juice

Heat a medium-sized wok or pot with olive oil over medium heat. Add the curry powder and stir for 3 seconds. Add the coconut milk, sugar, salt, peanut butter, and tamarind concentrate. Stir constantly until it returns to a boil, then turn off the heat immediately and continue stirring. Do not overcook, as the oil in the coconut milk will separate.

Keep warm and serve with yellow curry shrimp skewers, red curry salmon skewers or as salad dressing.

Serves 2.

GINGER SAUCE
(Jail King)

Either soy sauce or fish sauce can be used in this recipe, though using both is better.

1 tablespoon minced fresh ginger
1 clove garlic, minced
1 hot chili pepper, finely chopped (optional)
½ tablespoon fish sauce

½ tablespoon soy sauce
1 teaspoon sugar
1 teaspoon lime juice

Combine all of the ingredients in small sauce bowl and mix well. It tastes better if you add all of the ingredients in a mini-chopper, pulse 3 times.

It should taste spicy, sweet, and sour. It tastes best if refrigerated overnight.

Refrigerate in an airtight container for up to 3 weeks or freeze for up to 3 months.

Serves 2.

SWEET AND SOUR SAUCE
(Jail Some)

10 chili peppers
1 teaspoon brown sugar
1 tablespoon fish sauce

1 clove garlic
1 teaspoon lime or lemon juice

Combine all of the ingredients in a mini-chopper and pulse twice, scrape with spatula, and pulse one more time.

Refrigerate in an airtight container for up to 2 weeks or freeze for up to 3 months.

Serve in small sauce bowl with grilled fish or chicken.

Serves 2.

ROASTED TOMATO SAUCE
(Jail Mock Lent)

4 cloves garlic
2 shallots, halved or 1 small onion, sliced
2 large red hot peppers or ½ red bell pepper
(for mild version)

½ pound cherry tomatoes
¼ teaspoon salt
2 teaspoons fish sauce (optional)
¼ cup chopped cilantro

Place garlic, shallots, hot peppers, and tomatoes on a baking pan and broil in an oven or toaster oven until brown—about 8 minutes on each side.

Note: *the garlic and pepper might brown faster, so make sure to check them and take them out before they burn.*

Transfer the garlic, shallots, and hot peppers to a food processor. Pulse, scrape down the sides with a spatula, and pulse one more time. Scrape down with a spatula and add the tomatoes, salt, and fish sauce. Pulse two more times. It should be a little chunky. Add the cilantro and pulse once.

Serve as a dipping sauce with chicken, steak, or fish, or serve as a dip with steamed vegetables such as: cabbage, broccoli, zucchini, green beans, cauliflower, asparagus, or fresh cucumber.

Serves 4.

COLD
DISH

FRESH SPRING ROLLS WITH SHRIMP AND JICAMA
(Yall Dip Goung)

Be sure to wash your vegetables thoroughly and spin off the excess water.

10 pieces dried rice paper (spring roll skins)
¼ pound cooked shrimp, peeled, cleaned,
and cut lengthwise
¼ cup shredded carrot
1 cup finely sliced jicama

1 cup thinly sliced iceberg lettuce
½ cup chopped scallions
½ cup cilantro leaves
10 Thai basil or any basil leaves

Note: *If not serving immediately, wet a paper towel with cold water and place it over the spring rolls. Cover with plastic wrap and refrigerate for a few hours before serving. Making the rolls a day ahead of time is not recommended.*

Place all of the ingredients, minus the rice paper, on a tray (this can be done a day before). Get a large bowl of hot water from the faucet. You will need to change the water throughout the process as it cools.

Dip a sheet of rice paper in the water for 5 seconds, then let the excess water drip off for about 5 seconds. Carefully place the rice paper on a plate and straighten. Wait for a few seconds to allow the rice paper to get soft.

At the end nearest to you, place inside 2 pieces of shrimp and a pinch of shredded carrot, jicama, iceberg lettuce, scallions, cilantro, and basil. Do not add too much filling, as you will not be able to roll it nicely. Fold the end nearest to you over the ingredients and roll once. Fold the left and right sides toward each other so they meet in the middle and roll slowly, squeezing out the air. The rice paper should now be very soft and should glue itself. Serve with Peanut Sauce (page 20).

Serves 2.

FRESH SPRING ROLLS WITH CHICKEN AND BEAN SPROUTS
(Yall Dip Gice)

Be sure to wash all of the vegetables and spin off the excess water.

10 pieces dried rice paper (spring roll skins)
¼ pound roasted chicken, shredded
¼ cup shredded carrot
1 cup thinly sliced cucumber

1 cup fresh bean sprouts
¼ cup chopped scallions
¼ cup cilantro leaves
½ cup mint leaves

Place all of the ingredients, minus the rice paper, on a tray (this can be done the day before). Get a large bowl of hot water from the faucet. You will need to change the water throughout the process as it cools.

Dip a sheet of rice paper in the water for 5 seconds, then let the excess water drip off for about 5 seconds. Carefully place the rice paper on a plate and straighten. Wait for a few seconds to allow the rice paper to get soft.

At the end nearest to you, place inside 2 pieces of chicken and a pinch of shredded carrot, cucumber, bean sprouts, scallions, cilantro, and mint. Do not add too much filling, as you will not be able to roll it nicely. Fold the end nearest to you over the ingredients and roll once. Fold the left and right sides toward each other so they meet in the middle and roll slowly, squeezing out the air. The rice paper should now be very soft and should glue itself. Serve with Peanut Sauce (page 20).

Serves 2.

Note: *If not serving immediately, wet a paper towel with cold water and place it over the spring rolls. Cover with plastic wrap and refrigerate for a few hours before serving. Making the rolls a day ahead of time is not recommended.*

GREEN PAPAYA SALAD
(Tum Mock Houng)

Papaya salad is signature Lao dish. It is sold by street vendors, at fairs, and served at holiday events. Get-togethers always include Green Papaya Salad—as an afternoon snack to keep you awake or as a midnight snack to keep you up longer to enjoy the party. Most people like this dish to be very spicy.

1 pound green papaya
1 small chili pepper, finely chopped
(more or less to taste)
1 clove garlic, minced
¼ teaspoon salt
1 tablespoon fish sauce

1 teaspoon sugar
1 teaspoon lime juice
10 cherry tomatoes, thinly sliced
1 tablespoon chopped roasted peanuts
2 tablespoons coarsely chopped cilantro

Peel and shred the papaya (you should have about ½ pound of shredded fruit) and place in a mixing bowl. Add the chili peppers, garlic, salt, fish sauce, sugar, lime juice, and tomatoes. Mix with both hands (use gloves if desired), mixing and squeezing at the same time until all of the ingredients are well mixed and soft—about 10 times. Add the peanuts and cilantro, mix lightly, and serve at room temperature.

Serve as an appetizer or as a side dish with grilled chicken or fish.

Serves 2.

GREEN MANGO SALAD
(Tum Mock Muang)

When mangos are in season, Lao women get together and enjoy this dish for an afternoon snack. Make sure to buy a very green and hard mango. Always taste the mango prior to making the salad. If it is too tart, increase the amount of sugar; if it is too sweet, cut down or omit the sugar and add lime juice.

1 large green mango
1 small chili pepper, finely chopped
(more or less to taste)
1 clove garlic, minced
½ teaspoon salt

2 teaspoons fish sauce
2 teaspoons brown sugar
10 grape tomatoes, thinly sliced
2 tablespoons coarsely chopped cilantro

Peel and shred the mango (you should have about ¾ pound of shredded fruit). Transfer to a mixing bowl and add the chili pepper, garlic, salt, fish sauce, sugar, and tomatoes. Mix well with your hands (use gloves if desired). Add the cilantro, mix lightly, and serve at room temperature. Serve as an appetizer or side dish with grilled chicken and rice.

Serves 2.

ORANGE SHRIMP SALAD
(Yum Goung)

½ pound extra large shrimp, peeled and cleaned

1 teaspoon olive oil

1 clove garlic, minced

¼ teaspoon salt

¼ teaspoon black pepper

1 ½ medium oranges

1 chili pepper, finely chopped (optional)

2 teaspoons fish sauce

1 tablespoon lime juice

2 tablespoons finely sliced, fresh ginger

1 endive, cut in half lengthwise and thinly sliced at an angle

2 tablespoons coarsely chopped scallions

2 tablespoons coarsely chopped cilantro

2 tablespoons roasted cashew nuts, cracked

Combine in a mixing bowl: shrimp, olive oil, garlic, salt, black pepper, grated zest of the half orange, and juice of ¼ orange. Mix well and marinate for 10 minutes.

Preheat a grill pan over high heat, brushing or spraying it with oil. Grill the shrimp over high heat for 2 minutes on each side. Transfer to a large mixing bowl and let cool for 5 minutes.

Peel and cut 1 orange into ½ inch cubes and add to the shrimp. Add the juice of the remaining ¼ orange, the chili pepper, fish sauce, lime juice, and ginger; mix well. Add the endive, scallions, and cilantro; mix lightly. Sprinkle with the cashew nuts and serve cold or at room temperature.

Serves 2.

GRILLED VEGETABLE SALAD
(Yum Ping Puck)

2 portobello mushrooms

10 large asparagus

½ yellow bell pepper

½ red bell pepper

1 tablespoon olive oil

¼ teaspoon salt

¼ teaspoon black pepper

2 teaspoons fish sauce or soy sauce

2 teaspoons lime or lemon juice

2 tablespoons coarsely chopped scallions

2 tablespoons coarsely chopped cilantro

Preheat a barbeque grill on high, spraying or brushing it with oil. In a large bowl, combine the mushrooms, asparagus, and the yellow and red peppers. Add the olive oil, salt, and black pepper. Mix well and grill on high heat for 5 minutes on each side, except for the asparagus, which should only cook for 2 minutes on each side. Let cool and cut the mushrooms and peppers into ½ inch slices. Cut the asparagus in half. Add the fish sauce and lime juice and mix well. Add the scallions and cilantro, mix thoroughly, and serve cold or at room temperature.

Serves 2.

CELLOPHANE NOODLES WITH CHICKEN AND SPINACH
(Yum Sen Rorn Gice)

1 package (1.70 oz.) cellophane noodles
2 cups low fat, low sodium chicken broth
¼ pound chicken breast
½ teaspoon salt
½ pound (8 oz.) firm tofu, cut in ¼ inch cubes
6 oz. baby spinach leaves

2 teaspoons fish sauce
½ teaspoon hot pepper flakes (optional)
1 tablespoon lime juice
¼ cup thinly sliced red onion
2 tablespoons coarsely chopped cilantro

Soak the noodles in warm water for 10 minutes. Drain and cut into 4-inch strips.

In a medium pot, bring the chicken broth to a boil over high heat. Add the chicken and ¼ teaspoon salt. Return to a boil and cook for 8 minutes. Take the chicken out and let it cool. Keep the broth boiling, add the tofu, and return the broth to a boil. Add the noodles and turn off the heat. Add the spinach, stirring well (it cooks immediately). Drain quickly and transfer the mixture to a mixing bowl (reserving the broth for other uses). The noodles should absorb most of the liquid with about ½ cup remaining. Let the mixture cool for 10 minutes.

Shred the chicken with your hands and add to the noodles, mixing well. Add the remaining salt as well as the fish sauce, hot pepper flakes, lime juice, and onion; mix well. Add the cilantro and mix lightly. Serve cold or at room temperature.

Serves 2.

SEAFOOD SALAD
(Yum Talay)

1 cup low fat chicken or seafood broth

½ pound frozen seafood mix, thawed and drained well

¼ teaspoon salt

2 teaspoons fish sauce

1 tablespoon lime juice

1 clove garlic, minced

1 chili pepper, minced or ½ teaspoon hot pepper flakes

2 teaspoons minced fresh lemongrass

1 cup coarsely chopped radicchio

2 tablespoons coarsely chopped scallions

2 tablespoons coarsely chopped cilantro

2 tablespoons coarsely chopped fresh mint

In a medium pot, bring the chicken broth to a boil over high heat. Add the seafood and bring back up to a boil. Drain and transfer to a mixing bowl, reserving the broth for other uses. Let cool and refrigerate until cold—about 30 minutes.

Add the salt, fish sauce, lime juice, garlic, chili pepper, and lemongrass; mix well. Add the radicchio, scallions, cilantro, and mint; mix lightly. Serve cold.

Serves 2.

CELLOPHANE NOODLES WITH TURKEY AND WATERCRESS
(Yum Sen Rorn Gice Guang)

1 package (1.70 oz.) cellophane noodles

¼ pound ground turkey

¼ teaspoon salt

1 cup low fat chicken broth

1 bunch watercress, cut into 2-inch pieces

2 teaspoons fish sauce

½ teaspoon coarsely chopped hot peppers (optional)

1 tablespoon lemon juice

2 tablespoons coarsely chopped scallions

2 tablespoons coarsely chopped cilantro

Soak the noodles in warm water for 10 minutes. Drain and cut into 4-inch strips.

Preheat a nonstick wok or pan (without oil) over medium heat. Add the ground turkey and salt, stirring constantly. To prevent large chunks, break them down while stirring. Cook for 8 minutes and let cool for 5 minutes.

In a medium pot, bring the chicken broth to a boil over high heat. Add the noodles and watercress (they cook immediately), mix thoroughly and drain immediately. Transfer the mixture to a mixing bowl. Add ¼ cup of the broth back to the mixture (reserving the remaining broth for other uses) and let cool for 5 minutes.

Add the turkey to the noodles and mix well. Add the fish sauce, hot peppers, and lemon juice; mix well. Add the scallions and cilantro; mix lightly. Serve cold or at room temperature.

Serves 2.

CELLOPHANE NOODLES WITH SHRIMP AND BOK CHOY
(Yum Sen Rorn Goung)

1 package (1.70 oz.) cellophane noodles

½ cup chicken or seafood broth

¼ pound shrimp, peeled and cleaned

½ pound bok choy or napa cabbage, thinly sliced

1 cup thinly sliced leek hearts

¼ teaspoon salt

2 teaspoons fish sauce

½ teaspoon chopped chili peppers (optional)

1 tablespoon lime juice

2 tablespoons coarsely chopped cilantro

Soak the noodles in warm water for 10 minutes. Drain and cut into 4-inch strips.

In a medium pot, combine the chicken broth, shrimp, bok choy, cellophane noodles, and leeks. Do not stir. The steam will cook the mixture without losing any of the nutrients or flavors. Cover and cook over medium heat for 5 minutes. Transfer to a large mixing bowl, mix, and let cool for 5 minutes.

Add the salt, fish sauce, chili peppers, and lime juice; mix well. Add the cilantro and mix lightly. Serve cold or at room temperature.

Serves 2.

LETTUCE-WRAPPED STRIPED BASS WITH CILANTRO AND TOMATOES
(Pun Pa)

Wash and spin all vegetables before cutting.

½ pound striped bass fillet or other whitefish

¼ teaspoon salt

¼ teaspoon black pepper

2 teaspoons soy sauce

2 heads green leaf lettuce

10 cherry tomatoes, halved

2 cucumbers, peeled, quartered lengthwise, and thinly sliced across

½ cup chopped scallions

1 cup cilantro leaves

1 cup mint leaves

2 bowls Peanut Sauce (page 20)

Preheat the oven to 370 degrees or the barbeque grill to high heat. Season the fish with salt, black pepper, and soy sauce. Place the fish on a baking pan and cook in the oven for 20 minutes, or place in a double square of aluminum foil, close all four sides, and cook on the barbeque grill (with closed lid) for 8 minutes on each side.

Arrange the vegetables on a large platter. Shred the fish in bite-sized pieces and place in the middle.

Each person should have a large plate and a small bowl of peanut sauce. To eat, make one bite at a time: Place half of a lettuce leaf on your plate, add tomato, cucumber, scallions, cilantro, mint, and a piece of fish. Pick it up with your hands, dip in peanut sauce, and take a big bite.

Serves 2.

LETTUCE-WRAPPED CHICKEN WITH MINT AND STAR FRUIT
(Pun Gice)

Wash and spin all vegetables before cutting.

½ store-bought roasted chicken

2 heads red leaf lettuce

1 cup bean sprouts

2 star fruit (cut into strips and sliced across)

or 10 grape tomatoes (halved)

½ cup chopped scallions

1 cup cilantro leaves

1 cup mint leaves

Peanut Sauce (page 20)

Arrange the vegetables on a large platter. Shred the chicken into bite-sized pieces and place in the center of the platter.

Each person should have a large plate and a small bowl of peanut sauce. To eat, make one bite at a time: place half of a lettuce leaf on your plate, add bean sprout, star fruit, scallions, cilantro, mint, and chicken. Pick it up with your hands, dip it into the peanut sauce, and take a big bite.

Serves 2.

TURKEY AND EGGPLANT PURÉE
(Pone Gice Guang)

This dish is very healthy and easy to make—and it tastes great.

4 cloves garlic

1 large shallot, halved or 1 small onion, sliced

1 large hot pepper (preferably red) or ½ red bell pepper

(for mild version)

1 cup chicken broth

¼ pound ground turkey

¼ teaspoon salt

½ pound Asian eggplant or any eggplant,

cut into 1-inch cubes

2 teaspoons fish sauce

2 tablespoons finely chopped scallions

2 tablespoons finely chopped cilantro

Place the garlic, shallots, and peppers on a double square of aluminum foil. Fold and close all four sides to make a package. Place over medium heat on the stove or on a high heat barbeque grill. Roast for 8 minutes on each side. Take off the heat and let it cool.

In a medium pot, bring the chicken broth to a boil over high heat. Split the ground turkey into 4 pieces and add to the pot. Add the salt, cover, and bring back up to a boil. Add the eggplant. Stir well, cover, and cook for 5 minutes. Let cool for 5 minutes.

In a food processor, combine the garlic, shallots, and peppers. Pulse, scrape the mixture down, and pulse once more. Add the ground turkey mixture, pulse, scrape the mixture down, and pulse once more. Add the eggplant, pulse, scrape the mixture down, and pulse once more (it should be chunky). Add the broth, fish sauce, scallions, and cilantro, and pulse once. Serve warm or at room temperature with rice and steamed vegetables.

Serves 2.

LOB

Lob is a traditional Lao dish. We serve lob on holidays, special occasions, and to welcome a special guest. It is one of the few dishes that is served with wine (Lao rice wine, Low Lao, to be exact). Lob is made with beef, chicken, fish, duck, or wild game. The most common meat used in lob is chicken or beef. To make lob, the meat has to be very lean and fresh. No fat or oil is allowed in a lob recipe. Rice powder is a very important ingredient in lob; it adds a unique smoky flavor and makes it distinct from any other Lao dish.

RICE POWDER
(Kao Kore)

Store-bought rice powder will not give your lob recipe that unique smoky flavor. You can easily make it yourself. I recommend that you make it outside on a barbeque grill because it creates a lot of smoke. I recommend you make enough rice powder to use for one year; you need 1 tablespoon of rice powder for 1 pound of meat.

Put ½ cup plain, uncooked rice in a small aluminum tray. Place the tray on the grill over high heat. Close the lid, stirring and shaking the tray every 10 seconds until the rice is dark brown for about 8 minutes. Remove from the grill and let cool completely. Transfer the rice to a coffee grinder and grind for about 15 seconds or until it turns to powder (you want the consistency of fine sand). Store in an airtight container for a few months or refrigerate for 1 year.

Makes ⅓ cup.

CHICKEN LOB WITH ARTICHOKE
(Lob Gice)

1 lemon

4 oz. frozen artichokes, thawed

½ pound ground chicken

¼ teaspoon salt

2 teaspoons fish sauce

½ teaspoon hot pepper flakes (optional)

1 tablespoon lime juice

1 teaspoon kalanga (galangal) powder

2 Kaffir lime leaves, finely minced

½ tablespoon rice powder

2 tablespoons finely chopped scallions

2 tablespoons finely chopped cilantro

2 tablespoons finely chopped mint

1 head green leaf lettuce

Pour 1 cup of cold water into a small bowl and add the juice of a whole lemon. Thinly slice the artichoke and add it to the lemon water. Leave it in the lemon water until ready to use. Drain and squeeze off the excess water before use.

Preheat a nonstick wok or pan (do not use oil) over medium heat. Add the chicken and salt, stirring and breaking down the meat constantly. Cook for 5 minutes, but do not allow the meat to brown or overcook. Transfer the ground chicken to a medium mixing bowl and let cool for 5 minutes. Add the fish sauce, lime juice, pepper, kalanga powder, Kaffir lime leaves, and rice powder and mix well. Add the artichokes and mix thoroughly. Add the scallions, cilantro, and mint. Mix lightly to avoid bruising the herbs. Place 3 leaves of lettuce on the serving plate, pointing out from each other. Transfer the chicken lob into the center of the platter. Serve at room temperature with rice and lettuce leaves.

Serves 2.

SHRIMP LOB WITH BEAN SPROUTS
(Lob Goung)

½ pound shrimp, peeled and cleaned

½ teaspoon salt

2 teaspoons fish sauce

1 tablespoon lime or lemon juice

1 red hot chili pepper, chopped (optional)

1 teaspoon kalanga (galangal) powder

2 Kaffir lime leaves, finely minced

½ tablespoon rice powder

1 teaspoon finely minced lemongrass

2 tablespoons chopped red onion

1 cup fresh bean sprouts

2 tablespoons finely chopped scallions

2 tablespoons finely chopped cilantro

2 tablespoons finely chopped mint

1 head escarole

Finely mince the shrimp crosswise or cut crosswise into 4 pieces. Transfer the shrimp to a food processor. Pulse, scrape down the mixture, and then pulse 2 more times (they should be chunky). Transfer to a preheated nonstick wok or pan over medium heat. Add the salt and ¼ cup water, stirring constantly for 3 minutes, but do not allow the meat to overcook or brown. Transfer the shrimp to a medium mixing bowl and let it cool for 5 minutes. Add the fish sauce, lime juice, chili pepper, kalanga powder, Kaffir lime leaves, rice powder, lemongrass, and red onions; mix well. Add bean sprouts, scallions, cilantro, and mint. Mix lightly to avoid bruising the herbs. Place the escarole leaves on a serving plate, pointing away from each other. Transfer the shrimp lob to the center of the platter. Serve at room temperature with rice and escarole leaves.

Serves 2.

RAW FISH LOB WITH LEMONGRASS
(Lob Pa)

½ pound fresh lean striped bass or tuna fillet

2 tablespoons lime or lemon juice

½ teaspoon salt

2 teaspoons fish sauce

1 tablespoon finely minced fresh lemongrass

1 red hot chili pepper, chopped (optional)

1 teaspoon kalanga (galangal) powder

2 Kaffir lime leaves, finely minced

½ tablespoon rice powder

2 tablespoons thinly sliced shallots

1 tablespoon thinly sliced garlic

¼ cup finely chopped scallions

¼ cup finely chopped cilantro

¼ cup finely chopped mint

2 endive

Cut the fish into ¼ inch strips or cut into small cubes. Pulse in the food processor. Scrape down the mixture along the sides and pulse 2 more times. Transfer to a mixing bowl. Add lime juice. Mix well and let sit for 3 minutes. Add the salt, fish sauce, lemongrass, chili pepper, kalanga powder, Kaffir lime leaves, rice powder, shallots, and garlic; mix well. Add the scallions, cilantro, and mint. Mix lightly to avoid bruising the herbs. Place the endive leaves on a serving plate, pointing away from each other. Transfer the fish lob to the center of the platter. Serve with sticky rice and endive leaves.

Serves 2.

TURKEY LOB WITH GREEN BEANS
(Lob Gice Guang)

On Thanksgiving, Lao people in the US butcher a turkey, grind the meat, and make lob.

¼ pound Asian long beans or green beans

½ pound extra lean ground turkey

¼ teaspoon salt

2 teaspoons fish sauce

1 tablespoon lime or lemon juice

½ teaspoon hot pepper flakes (optional)

1 teaspoon kalanga (galangal) powder

2 Kaffir lime leaves, finely minced

½ tablespoon rice powder

2 tablespoons finely chopped scallions

2 tablespoons finely chopped cilantro

2 tablespoons finely chopped mint

1 head radicchio

Thinly slice the Asian long beans crosswise, then blanch in boiling water. (Drop into boiling water, stir, and immediately drain. Transfer to cold water and drain well.)

Preheat a nonstick wok or pan (do not use oil) over medium heat. Add turkey, salt, and ¼ cup water, stirring constantly and breaking down the meat. Cook for 5 minutes, but do not allow the meat to brown or overcook. Transfer the ground turkey to a medium mixing bowl and let it cool for 5 minutes. Add the fish sauce, lime juice, pepper, kalanga powder, Kaffir lime leaves, and rice powder; mix well. Add the Asian long beans and mix thoroughly. Add the scallions, cilantro, and mint. Mix lightly to avoid bruising the herbs. Place the radicchio leaves on a serving plate, pointing away from each other. Transfer the turkey lob to the center of the platter. Serve at room temperature with rice and radicchio.

Serves 2.

YELLOW CURRY SHRIMP SKEWERS
(Satay Goung)

10 bamboo skewers, soaked in warm water
at least 10 minutes
10 extra large or jumbo shrimp
1 teaspoon yellow curry powder
$1/8$ teaspoon white pepper

$1/2$ teaspoon sugar
1 teaspoon fish sauce
1 teaspoon soy sauce
2 tablespoons coconut milk

Shell and clean the shrimp. Make 2 small slits crosswise on the stomach of each shrimp so they will be straight when skewered with the bamboo skewer. Place in a small bowl. Add the curry, white pepper, sugar, fish sauce, soy sauce, and coconut milk. Mix well, cover, and refrigerate for 30 minutes.

Preheat a grill pan over high heat on a barbeque grill or stovetop, spraying or brushing it with oil. Skewer the bamboo skewer through each shrimp lengthwise from tail to head. Grill for 2 minutes each side. You can also broil the skewers in the oven for 5 minutes on each side. Serve hot with warm Satay Sauce (page 20).

Serves 2.

RED CURRY SALMON SKEWERS
(Satay Pa)

10 bamboo skewers, soaked in warm water as least 10 minutes

½ pound salmon fillet

1 teaspoon red curry paste

⅛ ground black pepper

½ teaspoon brown sugar

1 teaspoon fish sauce

1 teaspoon soy sauce

2 tablespoons coconut milk

Cut the salmon into 10 strips, ½ inch thick, 1 inch wide and 3 or 4 inches long. Place them in a small bowl. Add the curry, black pepper, sugar, fish sauce, soy sauce, and coconut milk. Mix well, cover, and refrigerate for 30 minutes.

Preheat a grill pan over high heat on a barbeque grill or stovetop, spraying or brushing it with oil. Skewer the bamboo skewers though each salmon strip lengthwise. Grill for 3 minutes on each side. You can also broil the skewers in the oven for 8 minutes on each side. Serve hot with warm Satay Sauce (page 20).

Serves 2.

GINGER-MINT SHRIMP DUMPLINGS
(Wonton Goung)

¼ pound medium shrimp, shelled and cleaned

½ teaspoon sesame oil

½ teaspoon hot sauce

½ teaspoon finely minced fresh ginger

1 tablespoon finely chopped shallots

1 tablespoon finely chopped mint

A pinch of salt

A pinch of black pepper

1 teaspoon soy sauce

10 wonton or dumpling wrappers, square or round

1 egg

4 collard greens leaves to keep dumplings from sticking to the steamer

Sauce

Mix together:

1 teaspoon soy sauce

½ teaspoon sesame oil

½ teaspoon finely minced ginger

1 teaspoon rice vinegar

2 tablespoons water

1 teaspoon finely chopped mint

Combine in a mini-chopper the shrimp, sesame oil, hot sauce, ginger, shallots, mint, salt, pepper, and soy sauce. Pulse twice, scrape down the mixture, and pulse one more time. Transfer to a mixing bowl and mix well.

Place 1 wonton wrapper on a plate and brush the sides with egg. Spoon ½ tablespoon of the shrimp mixture into the center of the wrapper. Pick up one corner of the wrapper and fold to the opposite corner to make a triangle or a half moon if wrapper is round. Press the edges to seal.

Line the steamer tray with 2 collard greens, then put a single layer of dumplings on the leaves. Do not let the dumplings touch each other or else brush them with oil to prevent them from sticking to each other. Place the left over 2 collard greens leaves on top of the dumplings and then another layer of dumplings. (Make two layers in each steamer, dividing them with leaves.) Steam over high heat for 10 minutes, then place on serving plate, drizzle with sauce, and serve hot.

Serves 4.

SPICY TURKEY DUMPLINGS
(Wonton Gice Guang)

¼ pound ground turkey

½ teaspoon sesame oil

¼ teaspoon hot sauce (more or less to taste)

½ teaspoon finely minced fresh ginger

1 tablespoon finely chopped scallions

1 tablespoon finely chopped cilantro

A pinch of salt

A pinch of black pepper

1 teaspoon soy sauce

10 wonton or dumpling wrappers, square or round

1 egg

4 collard greens leaves to keep dumplings from sticking to the steamer

Sauce Mix together:

1 teaspoon soy sauce

½ teaspoon sesame oil

½ teaspoon finely minced ginger

1 teaspoon rice vinegar

2 tablespoons water

1 teaspoon finely chopped cilantro

Combine in a bowl the ground turkey, sesame oil, hot sauce, ginger, scallions, cilantro, salt, pepper, and soy sauce; mix well.

Place 1 wonton wrapper on a plate, brushing the sides with egg. Spoon ½ tablespoon of the turkey mixture into the center of the wrapper. Pick up one corner of the wrapper and fold to the opposite corner to make a triangle or a half moon if wrapper is round. Press the edges to seal.

Line the steamer tray with 2 collard greens, then put a single layer of dumplings on the leaves. Do not let the dumplings touch each other or else brush them with oil to prevent them from sticking to each other. Place the left over 2 collard greens leaves on top of the dumplings and then another layer of dumplings. (Make two layers in each steamer, dividing them with leaves.) Steam over high heat for 10 minutes, then place on serving plate, drizzle with sauce, and serve hot.

Serves 4.

FRIED SPRING ROLLS WITH SHRIMP AND JICAMA
(Yall Jeune Goung)

1 package (1.7 oz.) cellophane noodles

1 cup shredded carrots

½ pound jicama, sliced in ¼ inch strips

½ pound medium shrimp

½ teaspoon salt

¼ teaspoon ground black pepper

1 tablespoon soy sauce

1 cup coarsely chopped scallions

1 package (25 pieces) frozen spring roll wrappers (spring roll shells or spring roll pastry), thawed

1 small egg for gluing

2 cups vegetable oil for frying

Soak cellophane noodles in warm water for 10 minutes; drain well and cut into 4-inch strips.

Preheat a wok or large pan over high heat without oil. Add the carrots, jicama, shrimp, salt, black pepper, and soy sauce, stirring constantly for 3 minutes. There should be some liquid from the vegetables. Add the cellophane noodles and scallions, stirring constantly for 2 minutes. The noodles should absorb all of the liquid. Transfer the mixture to a tray and spread it out to cool completely.

Place one wrapper on a flat surface, pointing one corner toward you. Brush the opposite corner with the egg wash. Spoon 2 tablespoons of the shrimp mixture onto the corner nearest you. Fold that corner over the mixture, roll it once, then fold the left and right corners toward each other so they meet in the middle. Continue rolling all the way to the end. Makes 20 rolls.

Preheat a frying pan or shallow pot with oil over high heat at about 375 degrees. Fry the spring rolls for 3 minutes on each side or until golden brown. Place the fried rolls on paper towels to absorb the excess oil. Serve hot by itself or with Peanut Sauce (page 20).

Serves 6.

FRIED SPRING ROLLS WITH CHICKEN AND SWEET POTATOES
(Yall Jeune Gice)

This dish needed a little bit of sweetness, so I added jicama for its natural sweetness and crunch and sweet potatoes for its natural sweetness and bright orange color.

1 package (1.70 oz.) cellophane noodles
½ pound ground chicken
1 medium onion, coarsely diced
½ pound, coarsely diced sweet potatoes
½ pound jicama, sliced in ½ inch strips
½ teaspoon salt

¼ teaspoon ground black pepper
1 tablespoon soy sauce
1 package (25 pieces) frozen spring roll wrappers
(spring roll shells or spring roll pastry), thawed
1 small egg for gluing
2 cups vegetable oil for frying

Soak cellophane noodles in warm water for 10 minutes; drain well and cut into 3-inch strips.

In a large mixing bowl, combine the noodles, ground chicken, onions, sweet potatoes, jicama, salt, black pepper, and soy sauce. Mix well with both hands (use gloves if desired).

Lightly beat the egg in a small bowl to use as glue. Place one wrapper on a flat surface, pointing one corner toward you. Brush the opposite corner with the egg wash. Spoon 2 tablespoons of the chicken mixture onto the corner nearest you. Fold that corner over the mixture, roll it once, then fold the left and right corners toward each other so they meet in the middle. Continue rolling all the way to the end. Makes 20 rolls.

Preheat a frying pan or shallow pot with oil over high heat at about 375 degrees. Fry the spring rolls for about 5 minutes on each side or until golden brown. Place the fried rolls on paper towels to absorb the excess oil. Serve hot by itself or with Peanut Sauce (page 20).

Serves 6.

COCONUT SOUP WITH BAY SCALLOPS
(Tome Ka Hoy)

4 slices fresh or dried kalanga (galangal)

1 stalk fresh lemongrass, cut in 2-inch pieces

2 Kaffir lime leaves (optional)

1 cup chicken broth

1 cup coconut milk

¼ pound bay scallops

4 oz. firm tofu, cut in ¼ inch cubes

½ cup sliced fresh button mushrooms

½ teaspoon salt

2 teaspoons fish sauce

2 tablespoons coarsely chopped scallions

2 tablespoons coarsely chopped cilantro

2 tablespoons lime or lemon juice

In a medium pot, add 2 cups of water as well as the kalanga, lemongrass, Kaffir lime leaves, and chicken broth. Bring to a boil over high heat. Cover and simmer for 30 minutes (it will reduce to about 1 cup). Discard the kalanga, lemongrass, and Kaffir lime leaves. Add the coconut milk and bring back up to a boil. Add the scallops, tofu, mushrooms, salt and fish sauce. Return to a boil and cook for 1 minute. Add the scallions, stirring well, and then turn off the heat. Add the cilantro and lime juice; serve hot.

Serves 2.

FISH SOUP WITH GREEN TOMATOES
(Gang Pa Mock Lent Dip)

If lemon basil (puck e tou) is not available, omit it. Do not substitute with any other kind of basil; it will not have the same flavor. Green tomatoes have a soft, sour taste that pairs well with lemon basil.

2 cups fish or chicken broth
1 stalk fresh lemongrass, cut in 2-inch pieces
or 1 tablespoon dried
3 slices fresh or dried kalanga (galangal)
2 Kaffir lime leaves
¼ pound striped bass or any other whitefish,
cut in bite-size pieces

½ teaspoon salt
½ tablespoon fish sauce
1 medium green tomato, cubed in ½ inch pieces
1 small onion, coarsely chopped
2 tablespoons coarsely chopped scallions
¼ cup lemon basil leaves or coarsely chopped cilantro

In a medium pot, add 1 cup of water as well as the fish broth, lemongrass, kalanga, and Kaffir lime leaves. Bring to a boil over high heat. Cover and simmer for 30 minutes (it will reduce to about 2 cups). Discard the lemongrass, kalanga, and Kaffir lime leaves. Bring the mixture back up to a boil. Add the fish, salt, and fish sauce; return to a boil. Add the tomatoes and onion; return to a boil. Add the scallions and lemon basil. Stir well and serve hot by itself, with rice, or with Raw Fish Lob (page 41).

Serves 2.

LEMONGRASS SOUP WITH RED SNAPPER
(Tome Yum Pa)

2 cups seafood or chicken broth
1 stalk fresh lemongrass, cut in 4 pieces
or 2 tablespoons dried
2 slices fresh or dried kalanga (galangal) (optional)
2 Kaffir lime leaves (optional)
¼ pound red snapper fillet or any whitefish,
cut in ¼ inch cubes
¼ pound coarsely chopped cauliflower

¼ teaspoons salt
1 tablespoon fish sauce
½ teaspoon chili and garlic paste or hot sauce
(more or less to taste)
2 tablespoons coarsely chopped scallions
2 tablespoons coarsely chopped cilantro
2 tablespoons tamarind concentrate or lime juice

In a medium pot, add 1 cup of water as well as the seafood broth, lemongrass, kalanga, and Kaffir lime leaves. Bring to a boil. Cover and simmer for 30 minutes (it will reduce to about 2 cups). Discard the lemongrass, kalanga and Kaffir lime leaves. Turn the heat high and bring to a boil. Add fish, cauliflower, salt, fish sauce, and chili paste. Return to a boil and cook for 1 minute. Add scallions, cilantro, and tamarind concentrate. Serve hot.

Serves 2.

LEMONGRASS SOUP WITH SEAFOOD
(Tome Yum Talay)

2 cups seafood or chicken broth

1 stalk fresh lemongrass, cut in 4 pieces

or 2 tablespoons dried

2 slices fresh or dried kalanga (galangal) (optional)

2 Kaffir lime leaves (optional)

¼ pound shiitake mushrooms, finely sliced

½ pound frozen seafood mix, thawed and drained

¼ teaspoon salt

1 tablespoon fish sauce

½ teaspoon chili and garlic paste or hot sauce

(more or less to your taste)

2 tablespoons coarsely chopped scallions

2 tablespoons coarsely chopped cilantro

2 tablespoons lime or lemon juice

In a medium pot, add 1 cup water as well as the seafood broth, lemongrass, kalanga, and Kaffir lime leaves. Bring to a boil over high heat. Cover and simmer for 30 minutes until reduced to 2 cups. Discard lemongrass, kalanga, and Kaffir lime leaves. Bring back up to a boil and add the mushrooms, seafood, salt, fish sauce, and chili paste. Return to a boil and cook for 1 minute. Add the scallions. Stir well and turn off the heat. Add the cilantro and lime juice; serve hot.

Serves 2.

WATERCRESS SOUP
(Gang Puck Num)

2 cups low fat, low sodium chicken broth

½ pound chicken breast, cut into ½ inch cubes

½ teaspoon salt

¼ pound (8 oz.) firm tofu, cut in ½ inch cubes

1 bunch watercress, coarsely chopped

2 stalks scallions, coarsely chopped

2 tablespoons coarsely chopped cilantro

In a medium pot, add the chicken broth and bring it to a boil on high heat. Add the chicken and salt. Return to a boil and cook for 3 minutes. Add the tofu and watercress; return to a boil. Add the scallion and cilantro; serve hot. Serves 2.

ROASTED HERBS FISH SOUP
(Tome Jail Pa)

1 inch fresh ginger, sliced across the grain into 4 pieces
1 stalk fresh lemongrass,
cut into 2-inch pieces across the grain
6 cloves garlic
2 shallots, halved or 1 small onion, sliced
1 long hot pepper or ¼ green bell pepper (for milder version)
2 cups chicken or fish broth
2 Kaffir lime leaves (optional)

¼ pound red snapper fillet or any whitefish,
cut in bite-size pieces
½ pound oyster mushrooms, shredded
¼ teaspoon salt
1 tablespoon fish sauce
¼ cup coarsely chopped leeks
2 stalks scallions, coarsely chopped
¼ cup coarsely chopped dill

Place ginger, lemongrass, garlic, shallots, and pepper on a baking pan. Broil in the oven for 8 minutes on each side or place in a double layer of square foil and cook in high heat on a barbeque grill for 5 minutes on each side.

Note: *the garlic and pepper might brown faster, so make sure to check them and take them out before they burn.*

In a medium pot, add 1 cup of water as well as the chicken broth, smashed ginger, smashed lemongrass, and Kaffir lime leaves. Bring to a boil over high heat and simmer for 30 minutes (it will reduce to about 2 cups). Discard the lemongrass and Kaffir lime leaves. Bring back up to a boil. Coarsely chop the garlic, shallots, and hot peppers in a mini-chopper or by hand and add to the pot. Add the fish, mushrooms, salt, and fish sauce. Return to a boil and cook for 1 more minute. Add the leeks, scallions, and dill; return to a boil. Serve hot by itself or with rice.

Serves 2.

FLAT RICE NOODLES WITH CASHEW NUTS AND TOFU
(Kore Mee, Pud Thai)

4 oz. dried flat rice noodles

2 tablespoons olive oil

4 cloves garlic, chopped

½ teaspoon hot pepper flakes

¼ pound chicken, sliced in bite-size pieces

1 teaspoon salt

¼ pound firm tofu, cut in ½ inch cubes

1 cup thinly sliced jicama

¼ teaspoon black pepper

1 tablespoon thick soy sauce

¾ cup chicken broth

1 cup sliced purple cabbage

¼ cup thinly sliced leeks

1 tablespoon roasted cashew nuts, crushed

1 tablespoon lime juice

¼ tablespoons coarsely chopped cilantro

Soak the noodles in warm water for 30 minutes and drain.

Heat a wok with oil on high heat. Add the garlic and stir constantly for 30 seconds or until light brown. Add the hot pepper flakes and stir well. Add the chicken and salt, stirring until the chicken is about 50 percent cooked. Add the tofu, jicama, pepper, and thick soy sauce; stir well. Add the chicken broth and return to a boil. Add the noodles, stir well, cover, and return to a boil. Add the cabbage and leeks; stir thoroughly to cook for another minute. Add the cashew nuts, lime juice, and cilantro; mix lightly and serve hot.

Serves 2.

RICE NOODLES WITH FISH GRAVY

(Kao Pune Num Pa)

This is signature Lao dish. In my hometown, there were few stalls that sold this dish as a street food. It could be breakfast or an afternoon snack. At the open-air markets in the capital of Laos (Vientiane, Viengchan), there were numerous stalls selling this dish, each with different flavor such as chicken, pork, beef, or fish.

3 oz. rice or somen noodles

4 slices fresh ginger

3 hot chili peppers

6 cloves garlic

2 shallots

3 cups chicken broth

3 slices fresh or dried kalanga (galangal)

3 Kaffir lime leaves

1/3 pound tilapia fillet or any whitefish fillet

1 teaspoon salt

1 tablespoon fish sauce

Mix together:

1 cup finely sliced purple cabbage

1 cup bean sprouts

2 tablespoons coarsely chopped scallions

2 tablespoons coarsely chopped mint leaves

2 tablespoons coarsely chopped cilantro

RICE NOODLES WITH FISH GRAVY
(continued)

Add 4 cups of water to a medium pot and bring to a boil on high heat. Add the noodles, stir well, and bring to a boil. Turn the heat down to medium and cook for 5 minutes. Rinse the noodles with cold water and drain well for about 30 minutes. They should be firm and stick together.

Place the ginger, garlic, chili peppers, and shallots on a double layer of foil and wrap it tight. Place on a medium heat barbeque grill or a gas or electric burner; roast for 8 minutes on each side.

Smash the ginger and put it into a medium pot. Add 2 cups of water as well as the chicken broth, kalanga and Kaffir lime leaves; bring to a boil over high heat. Turn the heat down to medium and simmer for 30 minutes (it will reduce to about 3 cups). Discard the kalanga and Kaffir lime leaves. Add the fish, salt, and fish sauce and cook for 5 minutes. Remove the fish and let the broth simmer. Put the chili peppers, garlic, and shallots in a food processor. Pulse twice, scrape down the mixture, and pulse 2 more times. Add the fish and pulse 3 times. Add the mixture to the broth and return to a boil.

Set out 2 large bowls and add half of the noodle with vegetable mixture and half of the fish gravy to each.

Note: *Mix each bowl well. The vegetables should still be crisp and the broth should be hot.*

Serves 2.

RED CURRY NOODLES
(Kao Pune Num Pik)

This is a signature Lao noodle dish. These noodles are freshly made every morning. By the end of the day, every single noodle must be sold and eaten.

3 oz. rice or somen noodles
6 slices dried or fresh kalanga (galangal)
4 Kaffir lime leaves
1 cup chicken broth
1 tablespoon olive oil
1 tablespoon red curry paste
1 teaspoon salt
1 tablespoon fish sauce (optional)
1 teaspoon sugar

1/3 pound ground turkey
1 can (13.5 oz.) coconut milk

Mix together:
1 cup coarsely chopped red and green leaf lettuce
1/2 cup shredded carrots
2 tablespoons coarsely chopped scallions
2 tablespoons coarsely chopped mint leaves
2 tablespoons coarsely chopped cilantro

In a medium pot, bring 2 quarts water to a boil over high heat in a medium pot. Add the noodles; stir well, and bring to a boil. Turn the heat down to medium, cook for 5 minutes, stirring occasionally. Rinse the noodles with cold water and drain well for about 30 minutes.

In a medium pot, add 1 cup of water as well as the kalanga, Kaffir lime leaves, and chicken broth; bring to a boil over high heat. Reduce the heat to medium and simmer for 30 minutes (it will reduce to about 1 cup). Discard the kalaga and Kaffir lime leaves, keep the broth simmer until ready to use.

Preheat a small nonstick pan with oil over medium heat. Add the curry paste, stirring constantly for 2 minutes; add to the broth. Add the salt, fish sauce, and sugar; return to a boil over high heat. Place the turkey in a bowl, add some hot broth, and mix well. Add this mixture to the remaining broth in the pot. Return to a boil, add the coconut milk, and cook for 2 minutes.

Set up 2 large bowls. Add to each bowl one half of the noodles, vegetables mixture, and hot curry broth. Mix your own bowl well and enjoy.

Serves 2.

YELLOW CURRY NOODLES
(Kao Pune Gali)

3 oz. rice or somen noodles

1 tablespoon olive oil

½ tablespoon yellow curry powder

$1/3$ pound chicken breast, cut in bite-size pieces

1 teaspoon salt

1 teaspoon sugar

1 can (13.5 oz.) coconut milk

1 tablespoon fish sauce (optional)

1 cup chicken broth

¼ pound potatoes, peeled and cut in ¼ inch cubes

¼ pound carrots, peeled and cut in ¼ inch cubes

Mix together:

1 cup finely sliced green cabbage

1 cup finely sliced cucumber

2 tablespoons coarsely chopped scallions

2 tablespoons coarsely chopped mint leaves

2 tablespoons coarsely chopped cilantro

In a medium pot, add 4 cups of water and bring to a boil over high heat. Add the noodles, stir well, and bring back up to a boil. Turn the heat down to medium and cook for 5 minutes, stirring occasionally. Rinse the noodles with cold water and drain well for about 30 minutes.

Preheat a wok or medium pot with oil over medium heat. Add the curry and stir for a few seconds. Add the chicken, salt, and sugar, stirring constantly for 1 minute. Add the coconut milk, fish sauce, and chicken broth; stir well and bring back up to a boil. Add the potatoes, cover, and bring to a boil. Reduce the heat to medium and cook for 3 minutes. Add the carrots, recover, and cook for another 3 minutes.

Set up 2 large bowls and add half of the noodles, vegetable mixture, and curry broth to each bowl. Mix your own bowl well and enjoy.

Serves 2.

FLAT RICE NOODLE SOUP
(Pher)

4 oz. flat rice noodles (dried)

4 cups chicken broth

1 onion, quartered

2 inches fresh ginger, halved lengthwise

1 celery stalk

¼ teaspoon salt

½ pound chicken breast

1 tablespoon soy sauce

1 teaspoon sugar

1 cup fresh bean sprouts

2 tablespoons coarsely chopped scallions

2 tablespoons coarsely chopped cilantro

¼ teaspoon ground black pepper

2 teaspoons lime juice

Hot pepper to taste (optional)

Soak the noodles in warm water for 30 minutes and drain.

In a medium pot, combine 1 cup of water with the chicken broth, ginger, celery, and salt; bring to a boil. Add the chicken, turn the heat low and simmer for 10 minutes. Remove the chicken, let it cool, and shred it. Discard the ginger and celery. Add the soy sauce and sugar; keep the broth simmering until ready to eat. The broth should be reduced to about 3 cups when it is ready to use.

In another pot, bring 3 cups of water to a boil. Add the noodles; stir well and strain immediately. Set up 2 large bowls and add half of the noodles, chicken, bean sprouts, scallions, and cilantro to each bowl. Bring the broth to a full boil and add half to each bowl of noodles. Add the black pepper, lime, and hot pepper; mix well and serve hot.

Serves 2.

GRILLED GINGER-CHICKEN
(Ping Gice King)

4 chicken cutlets

2 tablespoons finely minced fresh ginger

¼ teaspoon black pepper

¼ teaspoon salt

2 teaspoons soy sauce

1 tablespoon olive oil

Place chicken in a plastic bag; add the ginger, pepper, salt, soy sauce, and olive oil. Let out the air, close the bag, and coat the chicken very well. Refrigerate for 30 minutes. Preheat the grill on high heat, brushing or spraying it with oil. Grill the chicken for 5 minutes on each side. Serve with rice, steamed vegetables, and Ginger Sauce (page 21).

Serves 2.

GRILLED LEMONGRASS-CHICKEN
(Ping Gice See Kice)

4 chicken cutlets

2 tablespoons finely minced fresh lemongrass

¼ teaspoon black pepper

¼ teaspoon salt

2 teaspoons soy sauce

1 tablespoon olive oil

Place chicken in a plastic bag and add the lemongrass, pepper, salt, soy sauce, and olive oil. Let out the air, close the bag, and coat the chicken very well. Refrigerate for 30 minutes. Preheat the grill on high heat, and grill for 5 minutes on each side. Serve with rice, steamed vegetables, and Roasted Tomato Sauce (page 22).

Serves 2.

SPINACH WITH CHICKEN AND LOADS OF HERBS
(Orm Born)

1 tablespoon minced fresh lemongrass

4 cloves garlic

1 shallots or 1 small onion, sliced

1 hot pepper or ½ green bell pepper (for milder version)

1 tablespoon minced frozen kalanga (galangal), thawed or 1 tablespoon powdered

2 Kaffir lime leaves, finely chopped (optional)

1 tablespoon olive oil

¼ pound boneless chicken breast, cut in bite-size pieces

¼ teaspoon salt

1 cup chicken broth

1 tablespoon fish sauce (optional)

½ pound chopped frozen spinach, thawed and drained

¼ cup coarsely chopped leeks

2 stalks scallions, chopped

¼ cup coarsely chopped fresh dill

In a mini-chopper, combine the lemongrass, garlic, shallots, hot pepper, kalanga and Kaffir lime leaves. Chop for 10 seconds, scrape down the mixture, and pulse twice.

Heat a medium wok or pot with oil over medium heat. Add the mixture. Stir constantly for 2 minutes or until light brown. Turn the heat up to high and add the chicken and salt; stir for 1 minute. Add the chicken broth and fish sauce; bring to a boil. Add the spinach and bring back up to a boil. Cover and simmer for 5 minutes; stir occasionally. Add the leeks, scallions, and dill; mix well, bring back up to a boil, and serve hot with rice.

Serves 2.

RED CURRY CHICKEN
(Gang Pit Gice)

1 ounce dried wood ear mushrooms

1 tablespoon olive oil

½ tablespoon red curry paste

¼ pound boneless chicken breast,
cut in bite-size pieces

¼ teaspoon salt

1 teaspoon sugar (optional)

1 cup coconut milk

2 Kaffir lime leaves (optional)

1 tablespoon fish sauce

¼ pound cauliflower, sliced

¼ pound asparagus, cut at an angle in 2-inch pieces

2 stalks scallions, coarsely chopped

½ cup Thai basil or any basil leaves

Soak the wood ear mushrooms in hot water for 30 minutes and cut into bite-size pieces.

Heat a wok or pan with oil over medium heat. Add the curry paste and mix well for about 30 seconds. Turn the heat up to high and add the chicken, salt, and sugar; stir well until the chicken is 50 percent cooked. Add the coconut milk, Kaffir lime leaves, and fish sauce; return to a boil. Add the wood ear mushrooms and return to a boil. Add the cauliflower and asparagus; cook for 1 minute. Add the scallions and basil; stir well. Serve hot with rice.

Serves 2.

GRILLED LEEK-MEATBALLS
(Ping Louk Seen)

There were no breadcrumbs in Laos because we did not have any bread. I used leeks in the place of breadcrumbs to keep the meat moist. Plus, the leeks add more flavor and are also good for you.

½ pound ground turkey

¼ teaspoon salt

¼ teaspoon ground black pepper

2 teaspoons soy sauce (optional)

2 cloves garlic, finely minced

1 tablespoon finely minced fresh lemongrass

¾ cup finely chopped leeks

1 tablespoon olive oil

Spray a grill pan with oil and place on the barbeque grill over high heat.

In a medium mixing bowl, combine the ground turkey, salt, pepper, soy sauce, garlic, lemongrass, and leeks. Mix well with your hands (use gloves if desired). Take a tablespoon of the mixture and form it into a ball. Repeat with the rest of the mixture. Brush the meatballs with oil and place on the grill pan. Close the barbeque lid and cook them for 5 minutes on each side or until brown.

Or you can spray a baking pan with oil, place the meatballs on the pan, and brush them with olive oil. Then broil them in the oven for 8 minutes on each side. Serve them with rice, steamed vegetables, and Roasted Tomato Sauce (page 22).

Serves 2.

YELLOW CURRY CHICKEN
(Gang Gali Gice)

1 tablespoon olive oil
½ tablespoon yellow curry powder
¼ pound boneless chicken breast, cut in bite-size pieces
¼ teaspoon salt
½ tablespoon fish sauce
1 teaspoon sugar (optional)

1 cup coconut milk
1 teaspoon sugar (optional)
$^1/_3$ pound new red potatoes, quartered
¼ pound baby carrots
8 pearl onions, peeled
2 stalks scallions, coarsely chopped
¼ cup cilantro, coarsely chopped

Heat a wok or medium pot with oil over medium heat. Add the curry powder and mix well. Add the chicken, salt, and sugar; stir well. Add the coconut milk and fish sauce and return to a boil. Add the potatoes, cover, and return to a boil. Reduce the heat to medium and cook for 3 minutes, stirring occasionally. Add the carrots and pearl onions. Cover and cook for another 3 minutes, stirring occasionally. Add the scallions and cilantro; stir well and serve hot with rice.

Serves 2.

STIR
FRIED

SPICY CHICKEN AND CABBAGE STIR-FRY
(Kore Galum)

1 tablespoon olive oil

4 cloves garlic, chopped

1 hot chili pepper, chopped

¼ pound chicken breast,
thinly sliced in bite-size pieces

¼ teaspoon salt

½ pound green cabbage, cut in ½ inch slices

2 teaspoon oyster or soy sauce (or both)

¼ cup chicken broth

10 cherry tomatoes, halved

¼ cup coarsely chopped scallions

¼ cup coarsely chopped cilantro

Heat a wok or pan with oil over high heat. Add the garlic and stir constantly for 30 seconds or until light brown. Add the chili peppers and stir well for 10 seconds. Add the chicken and salt, stirring constantly for 2 minutes or until the chicken is 80 percent cooked. Add the cabbage, oyster sauce, and chicken broth, stirring constantly for a minute. Add the tomatoes and scallions, stirring well for another minute. Add the cilantro; stir well and serve hot with rice and Sweet and Sour Sauce (page 21).

Serves 2.

STIR-FRIED SHRIMP AND ASPARAGUS
(Kore Nall Mike)

1 tablespoon olive oil

4 cloves garlic, chopped

½ teaspoon hot pepper flakes

¼ pound shrimp, peeled and cleaned

¼ teaspoon salt

1 pound asparagus, trimmed and
cut at an angle in 2-inch pieces

½ tablespoon soy sauce

½ cup coarsely sliced red onion

2 tablespoons coarsely chopped cilantro

Heat a wok pan with oil over high heat. Add the garlic and stir constantly for 30 seconds or until light brown. Add the hot pepper flakes, shrimp, and salt, stirring constantly until the shrimp is 50 percent cooked. Add the asparagus and soy sauce, stirring constantly for 1 minute. Add the onion; stir constantly and cook 1 more minute. Add the cilantro; stir well and serve hot with rice and Sweet and Sour Sauce (page 21).

Serves 2.

STIR-FRIED GINGER BEEF WITH NAPA CABBAGE
(Kore Puck Got Kao)

1 tablespoon olive oil

4 cloves garlic, chopped

1 tablespoon chopped fresh ginger

½ teaspoon hot pepper flakes

¼ pound lean beef, thinly sliced in bite-size pieces

¼ teaspoon salt

3 cups coarsely sliced Napa cabbage (Chinese cabbage), sliced crosswise

1 tablespoon soy sauce

½ cup coarsely sliced onion

¼ cup coarsely chopped cilantro

Heat a wok with oil over high heat. Add the garlic and ginger, stirring for 30 seconds or until light brown. Add the hot pepper flakes, stirring for a few seconds. Add the beef and salt, stirring well to cook the beef 50 percent. Add the Napa cabbage, soy sauce, and onion, stirring constantly for 1 minute. Add the cilantro; stir well and serve hot with rice and Sweet and Sour Sauce (page 21).

Serves 2.

STIR-FRIED CHICKEN WITH GREEN BEANS AND TOMATOES
(Kore Mock Tore)

1 tablespoon olive oil

4 cloves garlic, chopped

1 hot chili pepper, chopped

¼ pound chicken breast, thinly sliced in bite-size pieces

½ teaspoon salt

½ pound green beans, trimmed and cut at an angle (French-cut)

2 teaspoons soy sauce

½ teaspoon sugar

¼ cup chicken broth

10 grape tomatoes, halved

½ cup sliced red onion

½ cup coarsely chopped Asian celery or celery leaves

Heat a wok or pan with oil over high heat. Add the garlic and stir constantly for 30 seconds or until light brown. Add the chili peppers and stir for 10 seconds. Add the chicken and salt, stirring constantly until the chicken is 50 percent cooked. Add the green beans, soy sauce, and sugar; stir well. Add the chicken broth, cover, and cook for 3 minutes, stirring occasionally. Add the tomatoes, onions, and celery, stirring constantly for another minute. Serve hot with rice and Sweet and Sour Sauce (page 21).

Serves 2.

STIR-FRIED GREEN BEANS WITH FRESH DILL
(Kore Puck See Mock Tore)

This is a favorite of mine that I like to share with my paternal grandmother. We love fresh dill!

1 tablespoon sliced lemongrass, cut crosswise

4 cloves garlic

1 shallot, sliced

1 jalapeño pepper (optional)

1 tablespoon olive oil

¼ pound ground turkey

½ teaspoon salt

1 pound Asian long beans, cut in 1-inch pieces, or green beans cut in half

½ tablespoon soy sauce

½ tablespoon oyster sauce

½ cup chicken broth

½ cup diced red bell pepper

¼ cup coarsely chopped scallions

1 cup coarsely chopped fresh dill

In a mini-chopper, add the lemongrass and chop for 10 seconds. Scrape the mixture down and add the garlic, shallots, and pepper; pulse 2 more times.

Preheat a wok or frying pan with oil over high heat. Add the lemongrass mixture, stirring for 30 seconds or until light brown. Add the ground turkey and salt, stirring constantly until the turkey is 50 percent cooked. Add the green beans, soy sauce, and oyster sauce; stir well. Add the chicken broth, cover, and cook for 5 minutes, stirring occasionally. Add the red bell pepper and stir constantly for another minute. Add the scallions and dill; stir well and serve hot with rice.

Serves 2.

STIR-FRIED LEMONGRASS BRUSSELS SPROUTS
(Kore Puck See Galum Noy)

If you don't like Brussels sprouts, try this dish—you might change your mind!

1 tablespoon sliced lemongrass, cut crosswise

4 cloves garlic

1 small red onion, sliced

1 large hot pepper (optional)

1 tablespoon olive oil

¼ pound ground chicken

¼ teaspoon salt

½ pound Brussels sprouts, quartered

½ tablespoon soy sauce

½ tablespoon oyster sauce

¾ cup chicken broth

½ cup diced yellow bell pepper

½ cup finely sliced leeks

1 cup chopped fresh dill

In a mini-chopper, combine the lemongrass, garlic, red onion, and hot pepper; chop for 10 seconds, scrape down the mixture, and pulse twice.

Preheat a wok or large pan with oil over high heat. Add the lemongrass mixture, stirring for 30 seconds or until light brown. Add the chicken and salt, stirring constantly until the chicken is 50 percent cooked. Add the Brussels sprouts, soy sauce, and oyster sauce; stir well and add the chicken broth. Cover and cook for 5 minutes; turn the heat down to medium, stirring occasionally. Add the yellow bell peppers and stir constantly for another minute. Add the leeks and dill; stir well, and serve hot with rice.

Serves 2.

GROUND BEEF AND EGGPLANT STIR-FRY
(Kore Mock Kure)

Eggplant has to be cooked over high heat and just for few minutes. Young eggplants are sweet and tender, while mature eggplants are bitter.

My paternal grandmother and I loved to cook different dishes with eggplant. As soon as I arrived at her farm, I always wanted to pick her beautiful vegetables. She would always tell me to wait until lunchtime. She said, "We pick them and they go right to the pot." She was right: The vegetables were very sweet when freshly picked and thrown directly into the pot. I really miss spending time with her.

4 cloves garlic, chopped

1 small red onion, sliced

1 hot pepper or ¼ green bell pepper, sliced

1 tablespoon olive oil

¼ pound lean ground beef or ground turkey

¼ teaspoon salt

¾ pound Asian eggplants or any eggplant,
cut in bite-size pieces

½ tablespoon soy sauce

½ tablespoon oyster sauce

½ cup beef or chicken broth

¼ cup finely diced orange bell peppers

¼ cup finely chopped leeks

1 cup coarsely chopped Thai basil or any basil

In a mini-chopper, combine the garlic, onion, and pepper. Pulse once, scrape down the mixture, and pulse one more time.

Preheat a wok or frying pan with oil over medium heat. Add the mixture. Stir constantly for 30 seconds or until light brown. Add the ground beef and salt, stirring constantly until the beef is 50 percent cooked. Add the eggplant, soy sauce, and oyster sauce; stir well. Add the beef broth, cover, and cook for 3 minutes, stirring occasionally. Add the orange bell peppers and leeks; stir well and cook for another minute. Add the basil; stir well and serve hot with rice.

Serves 2.

GROUND CHICKEN AND CUCUMBER STIR-FRY
(Kore Mock Tang)

1 seedless English cucumber or ½ pound Kirby cucumber

1 tablespoon olive oil

4 cloves garlic, chopped

¼ pound ground chicken

¼ teaspoon salt

½ tablespoon soy sauce

½ tablespoon oyster sauce

½ teaspoon sugar (optional)

10 grape tomatoes, halved

2 tablespoons coarsely chopped scallions

2 tablespoons coarsely chopped cilantro

Peel and halve the cucumber lengthwise and slice it at an angle into ½ inch thick pieces.

Preheat a wok or frying pan with oil over high heat. Add the garlic and stir for 30 seconds or until light brown. Add the chicken and salt, stirring constantly until the chicken is 80 percent cooked. Add the cucumber, soy sauce, oyster sauce, and sugar; stir well for 3 minutes. Add the tomatoes and stir constantly for another minute. Add the scallions and cilantro, stir well, and serve hot with rice and Sweet and Sour Sauce (page 21).

Serves 2.

GROUND TURKEY AND ZUCCHINI STIR-FRY
(Kore Mock Ur Yao)

½ pound green zucchini
¼ pound yellow zucchini
1 tablespoon olive oil
4 cloves garlic, chopped
1 tablespoon chopped fresh ginger
1 hot chili pepper, chopped
¼ pound ground turkey

¼ teaspoon salt
½ tablespoon soy sauce
½ tablespoon oyster sauce
¼ teaspoon sugar (optional)
2 stalks scallion, chopped
¼ cup chopped cilantro

Slice the zucchini lengthwise into ¼ inch thick slices, then pile up the slices and cut at an angle to make ¼ inch strips.

Heat a wok with oil over high heat. Add the garlic and ginger, stirring constantly for 30 seconds or until light brown. Add the chili pepper and stir well. Add the ground turkey and salt, stirring constantly until the turkey is 90 percent cooked. Add the zucchini, soy sauce, oyster sauce, and sugar; stir constantly for 2 minutes. Add the scallions and cilantro; stir well and serve with rice and Sweet and Sour Sauce (page 21).

Serves 2.

SHRIMP AND CAULIFLOWER STIR-FRY
(Kore Galum Dalk)

1 tablespoon olive oil

4 cloves garlic, chopped

1 chili pepper, chopped

¼ pound shrimp, peeled and cleaned

¼ teaspoon salt

¾ pound cauliflower, cut in bite size pieces

½ tablespoon soy sauce

½ tablespoon oyster sauce

½ teaspoon sugar (optional)

10 cherry tomatoes, halved

¼ cup coarsely chopped red onion

2 tablespoons coarsely chopped cilantro

Preheat a wok or pan with oil over high heat. Add the garlic and stir constantly for 30 seconds or until light brown. Add the chili pepper and stir well. Add the shrimp and salt, stirring constantly until the shrimp is 50 percent cooked. Add the cauliflower, soy sauce, oyster sauce, and sugar; stir well. Add the tomatoes and red onion, stirring constantly for another minute. Add the cilantro; stir well and serve hot with rice and Sweet and Sour Sauce (page 21).

Serves 2.

HOT BEEF
(Kore Mock Pit)

1 tablespoon olive oil

4 cloves garlic, chopped

1 tablespoon chopped fresh ginger

¼ pound jalapeño peppers or any other hot peppers, coarsely chopped

½ pound lean ground beef

¼ teaspoon salt

½ tablespoon oyster or soy sauce (or both)

1 medium red onion, coarsely diced

¼ cup beef or chicken broth

½ cup Thai basil or any basil leaves

Preheat a wok or pan with oil over high heat. Add the garlic and ginger, stirring constantly for 30 seconds or until light brown. Add jalapeño peppers and stir constantly for 2 minutes. Add the ground beef, salt, and oyster sauce, stirring constantly until the beef is 80 percent cooked. Add the onion and stir for another minute. Add the broth and basil, stir well, and serve hot with rice.

Serves 2.

SEAFOOD

GARLIC-GINGER CALAMARI
(Kore King Pa Murk)

1 tablespoon olive oil
¼ cup thinly sliced fresh ginger
4 cloves garlic, chopped
½ pound frozen calamari rings, thawed and drain well
1 teaspoon fish sauce

1 teaspoon soy sauce
1 teaspoon oyster sauce
5 hot chili peppers, cut in half lengthwise (optional)
1 medium red onion, thinly sliced
1 medium yellow bell pepper, thinly sliced

Preheat a wok or pan with oil over high heat. Add the ginger and stir constantly for a minute. Add the garlic and stir constantly for 30 seconds or until light brown. Add the calamari, fish sauce, soy sauce, oyster sauce, and chili peppers, stirring constantly for 2 minutes. Add the onion and yellow bell peppers; stir for another minute and serve hot with rice.

Serves 2.

SEA BASS ROASTED IN COLLARD GREENS
(Knap Pa)

This dish is traditionally made using banana leaves. Since banana leaves are not readily available in U.S. supermarkets, I changed the recipe to use collard greens.

1 tablespoons minced fresh lemongrass

4 cloves garlic

1 shallot, sliced

1 jalapeño pepper, sliced, or
green bell pepper, chopped

2 teaspoons fish sauce

2 tablespoons coarsely chopped scallions

¼ cup coarsely chopped leeks

¼ cup chopped fresh dill

2 (¼ pound) sea bass fillets

4 collard green leaves

In a mini-chopper, add the lemongrass and chop for 20 seconds. Add the garlic, shallots, and pepper; pulse twice, scrape down the mixture, and pulse 2 more times. Transfer the mixture to a large mixing bowl. Add the fish sauce, scallions, leeks, and dill; mix well. Coat the fish with the mixture and wrap each piece with 2 collard green leaves. Place the fish on a double layer of aluminum foil, wrap it tight, and place over high heat on the barbeque grill for 10 minutes on each side, or roast the fish in a 375 degree oven for 30 minutes. Serve with steamed vegetables and rice.

Serves 2.

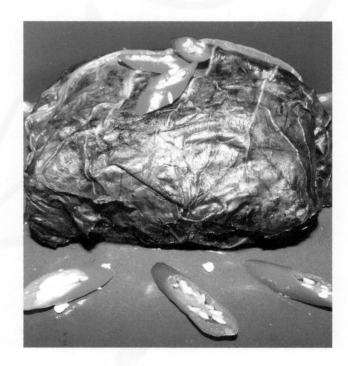

GRILLED GINGER-STRIPED BASS
(Ping Pa King)

2 (¼ pound) striped bass fillets

2 tablespoons finely minced fresh ginger

¼ teaspoon black pepper

1 teaspoon fish sauce

1 teaspoon soy sauce

1 teaspoon oyster sauce

1 teaspoon hot pepper flakes

1 tablespoon olive oil

Place the fish in a plastic bag. Add the ginger, black pepper, fish sauce, soy sauce, oyster sauce, hot pepper flakes, and olive oil. Let out all of the air and close the bag. Coat the fish very well and refrigerate it for 30 minutes. Preheat the grill to high, spraying or brushing it with oil. Grill the fish for 5 minutes on each side. Serve with rice, steamed vegetables, and Ginger Sauce (page 21).

Serves 2.

GREEN CURRY SALMON
(Gang Keo Pa)

1 tablespoon olive oil

½ tablespoon green curry paste

¼ pound salmon fillet, cut in 1-inch cubes

½ teaspoon salt

1 teaspoon sugar (optional)

1 cup coconut milk

2 Kaffir lime leaves (optional)

1 tablespoon fish sauce

¼ pound Asian Long Beans or green beans, cut in 1-inch pieces

¼ cup frozen peas, thawed

¼ pound asparagus, cut at an angle in 1-inch pieces

2 tablespoons coarsely chopped scallions

½ cup Thai basil or any basil leaves

Preheat a wok or pan with oil over medium heat. Add the curry paste and mix well for 30 seconds. Turn the heat up to high; add salmon, salt, and sugar and stir well. Cook for a minute, remove the salmon, and set aside. Add the coconut milk, Kaffir lime leaves, and fish sauce; return to a boil. Add the green beans; cover, return to a boil, and cook for 2 minutes. Add the peas, asparagus, and salmon; cover, bring to a boil, and cook for another minute. Add the scallions and basil; stir well. Serve hot with rice.

Serves 2.

YELLOW CURRY SCALLOPS
(Gang Gali Hoy)

1 tablespoon olive oil

½ tablespoon yellow curry powder

6 sea scallops

¼ teaspoon salt

1 cup coconut milk

1 tablespoon fish sauce

½ cup seafood or chicken broth

1 pound sweet potatoes, cut in ¼ inch cubes

6 pearl onions, peeled

2 stalks scallion, chopped

½ cup chopped cilantro

Preheat a wok or medium pan with oil over medium heat. Add the curry and stir for a few seconds. Add the scallops and salt, cooking for 1 minute on each side. Remove the scallops and set aside. Add the coconut milk, fish sauce, and broth; bring to a boil. Add the sweet potatoes and pearl onions. Cover and cook for 4 minutes, stirring occasionally. Add the scallops and bring to a boil. Add the scallions and cilantro; stir well and serve hot with rice.

Serves 2.

RED CURRY LOBSTER
(Gang Pit Goung Yice)

1 package (1.07 oz.) cellophane noodles
1 large (or 2 small) lobster
1 tablespoon olive oil
¼ tablespoon red curry paste
1 cup coconut milk
¼ teaspoon salt

1 teaspoon sugar (optional)
1 tablespoon fish sauce
2 Kaffir lime leaves (optional)
2 stalks scallion, coarsely chopped
½ cup Thai basil or any basil leaves
1 sprig of Thai basil or any basil

Soak the noodles in warm water for 10 minutes, then drain and cut them into 4-inch pieces.

Put the lobster in a large pot, adding 1 cup water. Cover, place on a high heat stove, and steam for 15 minutes. Let cool. Crack open the lobster, save the meat, and discard the shell. Cut the tail meat in half, lengthwise.

Preheat a wok or pan with oil over medium heat. Add the curry paste and mix for 30 seconds. Turn the heat up to high, then add the coconut milk, salt, sugar, fish sauce, and Kaffir lime leaves and return to a boil. Add the cellophane noodles and lobster; return to a boil. Add the scallions and basil and stir well. Transfer to a pasta bowl, garnish with sprig of basil, and serve hot with rice.

Serves 2.

DESSERTS

BUTTERNUT SQUASH CUSTARD
(Gati Mock Ur)

1 package (10 oz. frozen) cooked butternut squash
4 large eggs, beaten
½ cup sugar

½ teaspoon salt
1 cup coconut milk
1 tablespoon sesame seeds

Preheat oven to 350 degrees. Combine in a mixing bowl the butternut squash, eggs, sugar, salt, and coconut milk; mix well with whisk. Ladle the mixture into 8 medium soufflé cups, fill ¾ up. Place in a baking tray. Add water to the tray, fill ½ up and bake for 30 minutes. Let it cool for 10 minutes to serve warm or refrigerate 2 hours to serve cold.

Preheat small frying pan on high heat. Add sesame seeds, stirring and shaking constantly for 3 minutes. Transfer to a bowl and let cool. Sprinkle with sesame seeds before serving.

Serves 8.

COCONUT YUCCA
(Kao Nome Mun Tone)

1 pound yucca root

1 cup coconut milk

½ cup sugar

½ teaspoon salt

½ cup shredded coconut, dried

(sweetened or unsweetened) or frozen, thawed

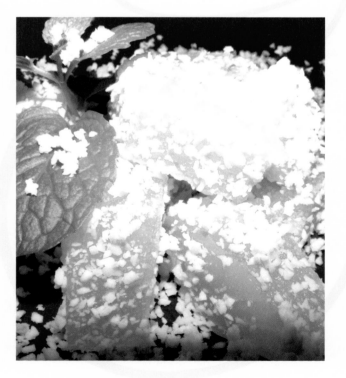

Preheat oven to 350 degrees. Peel yucca root and remove hard core from the center. Cut into small pieces, transfer to a food processor and chop until fine. Scrape down the mixture, add coconut milk, sugar, and salt. Chop until smooth for 2 minutes. Line the square baking pan with parchment paper and poor in the mixture. Spread evenly and bake for 30 minutes. Let it cool completely and cut into diamond shapes. Transfer to a mixing bowl, add shredded coconut and coat well. Serve at room temperature or cold.

Serves 6.

Note: *Frozen shredded coconut is ready to use after thawed; if using dried shredded coconut, chop in food processor until fine.*

COCONUT STICKY RICE
(Kao Mun)

1 cup sticky rice (sweet rice from Thailand)

2 tablespoons sesame seeds

1 cup coconut milk

½ teaspoon salt

½ cup frozen shredded coconut, thawed

½ cup sugar

Soak the rice in warm water for 2 hours and drain well before using.

Preheat frying pan on high heat. Add sesame seeds, stirring and shaking constantly for 3 minutes. Transfer to a bowl and set aside to cool.

In a medium pot, add coconut milk and ¼ teaspoon salt; bring to a boil over medium heat. Add rice and stir well; return to a boil, stirring occasionally. Reduce the heat to low, cover and simmer 8 minutes. Turn off the heat, stirring well and let sit for 5 minutes. Place shredded coconut in a mixing bowl. Add sugar and remaining salt and mix well.

Place a large ring on a serving plate. Fill with the rice about 1½ inch thick and spread evenly. Spoon 2 tablespoons of coconut on top the rice and spread evenly. Remove the ring, sprinkle with sesame seeds, and serve warm.

Serves 6.

MANGO STICKY RICE
(Kao Neal Mock Muang)

1 cup sticky rice
(sweet rice from Thailand)
1 ripe mango

1 cup coconut milk
½ teaspoon salt
½ cup sugar

Soak the rice in warm water for 2 hours and drain well before using. Peel the mango and slice across the grain. Keep cold in the refrigerator.

In a medium pot, add coconut milk and salt; bring to a boil over medium heat. Add rice, stir well, and return to a boil. Turn the heat to low, cover, and simmer for 8 minutes. Let it sit for 5 minutes. Add sugar, stirring well, and let it sit another 5 minutes. Transfer to serving a plate and flatten it evenly. Place mangos on top and serve warm.

Serves 6.

PUMPKIN PUDDING
(Mock Ur Gati)

1 cup coconut milk
1 package unflavored gelatin
½ cup sugar
½ teaspoon salt

1 can (15 oz.) pumpkin
1 egg, beaten
¼ cup shredded coconut, dried
(sweetened) or frozen, thawed

In a medium pot, combine the coconut milk, gelatin, sugar, salt, and pumpkin, and whisk well.

Place over medium heat and continue whisking until it comes to a boil. Continue whisking for another minute after boiling. Combine 1 cup of the mixture with the egg; whisk well and transfer the egg mixture back to the pot and continue whisking for another minute. Turn off the heat and continue whisking for 2 more minutes. Ladle the mixture into 8 glass bowls and refrigerate 2 hours.

If using dried shredded coconut, place in food processor and chop for 10 seconds. Sprinkle on top of the pudding and serve cold.

Serves 8.

SWEET POTATO SQUARES
(Gati Mun Gail)

15 oz. cooked sweet potatoes

⅓ cup rice flour

½ cup brown sugar

½ teaspoon salt

1 cup coconut milk

¼ cup shredded coconut, dried

(sweetened) or frozen, thawed

In a medium pot, combine the sweet potatoes, rice flour, brown sugar, salt, and coconut milk. Mix well with whisk. Place over medium heat and continue whisking 8 minutes until it comes to a boil. Continue whisking another 2 minutes after boiling. Turn off the heat and continue whisking another minute. Pour into a square pan lined with parchment paper. Spread evenly and refrigerate for 2 hours. If using dried shredded coconut, place in food processor and chop 10 seconds. Sprinkle on top and cut into squares and serve cold.

Serves 6.

Asian Celery (Sa Na Ly): Asian celery is one-tenth the size of American celery, but the aroma is much stronger. Asian celery has a lot of leaves and very small stems. If not available, use the leaves of American celery.

Basil (Bore La Pa): Basil has a wonderful and sweet aroma; I love this herb. Well, I love all herbs and vegetables. You can add basil to any stir fry, it will change the flavor, to a nice flavor. If you like it; knock yourself out. It smells good and is good for you. There are 3 kinds of basil in Laos: *See Cinnamon Basil/Thai Basil (Bore La Pa), Holy Basil (Puck E Tou Ka), Lemon Basil (Puck E Tou).*

Bean Sprouts (Tore Galk): Bean sprouts are typically sprouted from mung beans. Bean sprouts should look fresh and plump. They will only last a few days after you purchase them, though this depends on how long it has been since they were picked. If the bean sprouts were recently picked, they should last for about a week.

Bok Choy (Puck Got): There are many kinds of bok choy. They taste very similar, though, so you can use any variety in these recipes.

Cauliflower (Galum Dalk): Cauliflower was expensive in Laos because it didn't grow very well in that climate. It was also much smaller than those grown in the U.S.

Cinnamon Basil / Thai Basil (Bore La Pa): It is called Bore La Pa "borelapa" in Laos, Thai call it Hoh Ra Pa "Hohrapa." It is very popular in both Laos and Thailand. Basil has similar aroma to Italian basil, but the smell is sweeter; either one can be used.

Cellophane Noodles (Sen Rorn): Cellophane noodles are made from mung beans. They are easy to handle and do not easily break apart. Drop in boiling water or soup; they cook immediately. They are translucent after they are cooked. Wait five to ten minutes before serving; they will expand.

Chili Peppers (Mock Pit Noy): There are many varieties of chili peppers of all sizes and shapes. Typically the smaller the chili pepper, the hotter they are. For a milder flavor, use larger peppers that are not too spicy.

Cilantro (Puck Holm): Cilantro is also called coriander leaf and Chinese parsley. Cilantro has a very different aroma than parsley. Many people told me that they don't like it in Mexican food but that it's okay in my food. It is all about the right combination of herbs; give it a few tries because herbs are good for you. Cilantro is used in almost every dish in Lao cuisine.

Coconut (Mock Pao): Coconut is used in several different ways in Lao cooking. You can use the juice, the milk, and the cream. There is no cholesterol in coconut milk.

Coconut Juice: is the clear liquid from inside a young coconut. When the coconut is young, the meat is very tender and the juice is perfectly sweet. It is great for drinking and I recommend it when visiting a tropical country.

Coconut Milk: is made by finely blending mature coconut meat with warm water and then straining and squeezing out the milk. The brown coconuts that you find in the supermarket are mature coconuts. Coconut milk is used in Lao desserts 99 percent of the time; it is not a dessert without coconut or coconut milk.

Cream of Coconut: is concentrated coconut milk mixed with sugar.

Cucumber (Mock Tang Gore): The only species of cucumber grown in Laos is the Kirby cucumber. Personally, I like the flavor of Kirby cucumbers better than other cucumber species.

Curries (Gali): When you say the word *curry* by itself, it means *yellow curry powder*, originally made in India. The best quality and price of curry (yellow curry powder) is at Indian grocery stores. It tastes completely different from red and green curry paste. *See Green Curry and Red Curry for more detail.*

Dill (Puck See): Dill is very popular in Lao cooking; it is used fresh and in large amounts. It has a very strong flavor and does not go well with everything. A small amount of fresh dill will dramatically change the taste of the dish, so be careful not to get it in a dish where it is not called for. Fresh dill is sold in most supermarkets.

Eggplant (Mock Kure): There are many species of eggplant grown in Laos. Asian eggplants are sweet and tender and are preferred. Eggplants are used a lot in Lao cooking. They are mostly roasted, but some are steamed and some are fried. Some that are sweet and crunchy are served raw.

Fish Sauce (Num Pa): Fish sauce is made from salted fish that are fermented, then pressed to extract the liquid. When straight from the bottle, the flavor is very salty and fishy, but the fishy taste will fade once it is added to food, leaving only a nice flavor to the dish. If you don't like the taste, omit it and increase the salt.

Flat Rice Noodles (Dried) (Sen Pher): Flat rice noodles are typically steamed on a flat surface until they are partially cooked and then sliced and dried. There are a variety of widths of the flat noodles, which are used based on the recipe type and personal preference. I recommend size M.

Fresh Spring Roll Wrappers (Spring Roll Skins, Rice Paper) (Bai Yall Dip): Spring roll wrappers are made from rice or tapioca flour. They are steamed on a flat surface until fully cooked and then dried in bamboo weaves. When using spring roll wrappers, make sure to dip them in warm water to rehydrate them. They will become soft in just a few seconds.

Fried Spring Roll Wrappers (Spring Roll Shells, Spring Roll Pastry) (Bai Yall Jeune): Fried spring roll wrappers are made from wheat flour and are available in the freezer section, but they must be thawed as well.

Galangal (Ka): Galangal is also call Kalanga. *See Kalanga for more detail.*

Garlic (Puck Tiam): Lao cuisine uses a lot of garlic, especially roasted or fried garlic. When using raw garlic, stay with what the recipe calls for, but cooked garlic can be added as much as you want. So go crazy with cooked garlic; it will add a very nice flavor to your dish.

Ginger (King): Ginger is a root spice. I like to use fresh ginger, which is sold at most supermarkets. Fresh ginger will last for about three weeks on the counter. Don't get it wet. To extend the life of fresh ginger, wrap it in a paper towel and place it in a plastic bag in the refrigerator. It will last up to a month if refrigerated. Fresh ginger also freezes well.

Green Beans (Mock Tore): Both Asian long beans and string beans are available in Laos. Asian long beans can be over a foot long and are preferred for cooking, but string beans are a good substitute.

Green Curry Paste (Num Gang Pit Keo): Green curry paste is made from green pepper and many other spices; the color is green. It's spicier and tastes a little different from red curry paste, but it is very different from yellow curry powder. I recommend a four oz. can imported from Thailand.

Green Mango (Mock Muang Dip): Green mangos are usually sour, but sometimes you will find one that is sweet. Make sure to choose a very hard and green one to make the Green Mango Salad recipe found in this cookbook.

Green Papayas (Mock Houng): To make the Green Papaya Salad recipe found in this cookbook, you must use green papayas only. They are sold at any Asian grocery store. Make sure to pick one that is very green and very hard.

Green Tomatoes (Mock Lent Dip): Green tomatoes are great in soup. They add tartness and can be used in place of limes or lemons. They are not quite as sour as limes, though, so you will need to add a lot to taste the tartness.

Holy Basil (Puck E Tou Ka): Holy Basil has very unique aroma that not many people like and is not popular in Laos but very popular in Thailand. It is called Puck E Tou Ka in Lao; Thai call it Bai Gra Prow. It's usually used in stir fry; give it a try to see if you are the majority of people who don't like it or the minority that love it.

Hot Pepper Flakes (Mock Pit Pong): Hot pepper flakes found in the regular supermarket are made from dried and crushed peppers. They are not as hot as the hot pepper flakes found in Asian supermarkets. These flakes are typically made in Thailand, where the peppers are toasted and ground, giving them a finer, hotter flavor. If you like a lot of heat in your cooking, use hot pepper flakes from the Asian market.

Jicama (Mun Pow): In my hometown in Laos, jicama grows on land and they have the same texture as those you can find in the U.S., though they are not as big. In the capital of Laos, Vientiane (Viangchan), jicama grows in the sand by the Mekong riverbank. They are harvested young—about bite-sized—so they are tender and sweet, eaten as fruit. I like to use jicama in my recipes for its natural sweetness and crunch.

Jalapeño Peppers: There are many kinds of hot peppers in Laos, but jalapeño peppers do not grow there. Though not traditional, I like to use them for their mild spiciness and for the meatiness of the pepper. Though for me jalapeño peppers are mild, they may be too hot for some people.

Kaffir Lime Leaves (Bai Kee Hood): Kaffir limes grow in large trees and the skin has a bumpy texture, unlike the smooth skin of regular limes. The fruit of the Kaffir lime is not edible, though it is often used to wash hair for a healthy-looking shine. The leaves and zest, however, are often used in recipes. You can find Kaffir lime leaves fresh and frozen at Asian and gourmet grocery stores.

Kalanga (Galangal) (Ka): Kalanga is also call Galangal. It is a root spice that looks like ginger but it is harder and has a different flavor. It is available in dried, frozen, and powdered form at Asian and gourmet groceries.

Leeks (Bai Puck Tiam): I often use leeks in the place of garlic leaves, which are not available in the supermarket. I grow the garlic leaves myself in the summer; they are stronger than leeks and milder than garlic. When summer is over, I use leeks.

Lemongrass (See Kice): Dried lemongrass is good for soup; it is too hard for other uses. Most gourmet and specialty stores sell fresh lemongrass. Some nurseries sell potted lemongrass that you can grow yourself. It is easy to grow but it needs a lot of sun. If you buy it fresh, cut it 3 or 4 inches long, store in a plastic bag, and freeze it for later. Lemongrass is fibrous, so thinly slice across the grain and blend well in a blender before using in marinades. In Laos, it grows wild and is very inexpensive.

Lemon Basil (Puck E Tou): Lemon basil has a soft lemony aroma and is different from other basil, very popular in Laos and it's our signature herb. It is called Puck E Tou in Laos, Thai call it Mang Luck. Do not substitute with other kinds of basil. I love this lemon basil. My paternal grandmother grew a lot of it on her farm and they grew very big and tall. I miss her every time I smell or use lemon basil. She said to me, "We pick, wash and go right to the pot, we don't pick them and leave them around."

Lemons (Mock Nao Liung): Lemons are not commonly used in Lao cooking. Limes are preferred, but lemons are used when limes are not available. Lemon peel is thicker than lime, but if it feels a little soft, there is a lot of juice inside.

Limes (Mock Nao): Limes have a more refreshing taste than lemons, which is why Lao cooking prefers to use limes instead of lemons. The good news is that limes in the U.S. do not have seeds. Choose a lighter green lime to indicate that it's mature. Feel it. If it's little bit soft, it indicates that there is a lot of juice. If it's rock hard, there is no juice inside.

Mint (Puck Gan Gum): There are many kinds of mint in Laos and we typically use what's available. Mint is a must-have in Lob recipes. It is not a Lob without mint. It's great in salad and to refresh any dish.

Napa Cabbage (Puck Got Kao): Napa cabbage is also called Chinese cabbage. In Laos, Napa cabbages are much smaller than the ones found in the U.S. It has a very mild taste; it is very tender and has a lot of water, about 60 percent. Sauté on high heat and it will cook in just a few minutes; drop in hot soup and it will cook immediately.

Olive Oil: Olive oil is not available in Laos, but in the U.S. I use it in stir-fry recipes because it tastes good and is good for you. Do not use olive oil when deep-frying.

Oyster sauce (Num Mun Hoy): Oyster sauce is oyster flavor sauce made from oysters and salt. Any brand or low sodium kind will work fine. If you don't like the taste, omit it and increase the salt.

Red Curry Paste (Num Gang Pit Dang): Red curry paste is made from red pepper and many other spices; the color is red. It tastes similar to green curry paste and is very different from yellow curry powder. I recommend a four oz. can.

Rice Noodles (Kao Pune): Rice noodles are made from rice and are the same size as angel hair pasta. Rice noodles are Lao signature noodles. In Laos, rice noodles are freshly made every morning. By the end of the day, all rice noodles must be sold and eaten. They are used in **Red Curry Noodles, Yellow Curry Noodles,** and **Rice Noodles with Fish Gravy**. In Laos, these dishes sold at street vendors. If you visit Laos, please, enjoy them, everything is freshly made every single day.

Scallions (Puck Bore): Scallions are used in almost every dish in Lao cuisine and are a must-have in the refrigerator. The green part of the scallion is milder than the white part.

Shallots (Hore Puck Bore): Shallots are used often in Lao cuisine—we prefer to use shallots rather than onions. Roasting and frying shallots is very common in Lao cooking.

Somen Noodles (Kao Pune): Somen noodles are made from wheat. I use somen noodles because rice noodles are not always available in the supermarket. They are the same size and texture as rice noodles.

Soy Sauce (Sa Ew): Soy sauce is a soybean flavor sauce made from soy beans and salt. Any brand or low sodium kind will work fine. If you don't like the taste, just omit it and increase the salt.

Sticky (or Sweet) Rice (Kao Neo): When you purchase sticky (or sweet) rice, make sure the label says: sticky (or sweet) rice from Thailand. Not everyone has used sticky rice and it could be mistaken for the Japanese sweet rice used for making sushi.

Tamarind (Mock Kam): Tamarind grows in very large and tall trees in both sweet and sour varieties. One tree produces thousands of pieces of fruit. Sour tamarinds are used in cooking and eaten as a snack to stay awake, while sweet ones are eaten as fruit from India called Tamarind Concentrated from Thailand with a picture of tamarind fruit, it is sometimes called Concentrate Cooking Tamarind, Sour Soup Base Mix or Thai Fruit Concentrate.

Thai Basil (Bore La Pa): *See Cinnamon Basil*

Thick Soy Sauce (Sa Ew Dum): Thick soy sauce is sweet and used for its brown color. You will need to add salt to the recipe if using thick soy sauce.

Tofu (Tao Hou): Tofu is processed, fully-cooked soybeans. It has a lot of protein and no fat. There are a variety of textures available in tofu pertaining to firmness: silk, soft, firm, extra firm, and hard. Use whichever level of firmness that you prefer. Keep the tofu in the refrigerator in water, changing the water once a week. It will last for weeks this way. When marinating tofu, you need to use a hard tofu to keep the tofu from falling apart in the marinade.

Turmeric (Kee Min): Turmeric is used for its bright orange color. It is also very good for you, so now I like to use it even more.

Watercress (Puck Num): Watercress grows in water, so wash it thoroughly as there can be silt and small snails stuck in the stems. Watercress can be a little bitter if it is used fresh, though it loses the bitterness as it cooks. It will cook instantly when you drop it into boiling water or soup, so keep watch over it.

Wood Ear Mushrooms (Hit Sa Nune): Wood ear mushrooms grow wild in Laos, but they were often slimy. Farm-grown wood ear mushrooms are not slimy. Try to use the larger mushrooms, as the tiny ones are often slimy. They are sold at supermarkets but are very expensive in a little package; buy them at Asian grocery stores costing ten times less.

Wrappers (Bai Hall): Wonton and dumpling wrappers are made from wheat flour and are typically available fresh in many supermarkets and Asian grocery stores. Extra wrappers can be frozen for future use.

Yucca (Mun Tone): Yucca is a root vegetable, steamed or roasted for snacks or ground up to make Coconut Yucca for great desserts. You can find yucca in a Latin supermarket, fresh or frozen; I prefer fresh and peel it myself. I could not believe how plentiful yucca is in the U.S.A.

Zucchini (Mock Ur Yao): I use zucchini in place of young winter squash. Zucchini are so abundant here in the US, I use them in many of my recipes. I still use any kind of young winter squash whenever I find them.

For more detail of exact ingredients to be used, please check my web site www.laochef.com or
e-mail me at laotianchefs@aol.com

*Penn and Soutara Hongthong are donating a portion of
all proceeds to their charity,*

"help the Poor in Laos:"
www.helpthepoorinlaos.com

Healthy Lao Cuisine...

For more information regarding Penn Hongthong and her work,
visit her web site: www.laochef.com or
email her at laotianchefs@aol.com.

Additional copies of this book may be purchased online from
LegworkTeam.com; Amazon.com; BarnesandNoble.com; Borders.com,
or via the author's web site: www.laochef.com.

You can also obtain a copy of the book by visiting L.I. Books or
ordering it from your favorite bookstore.

Printed in the United States
150637LV00001B